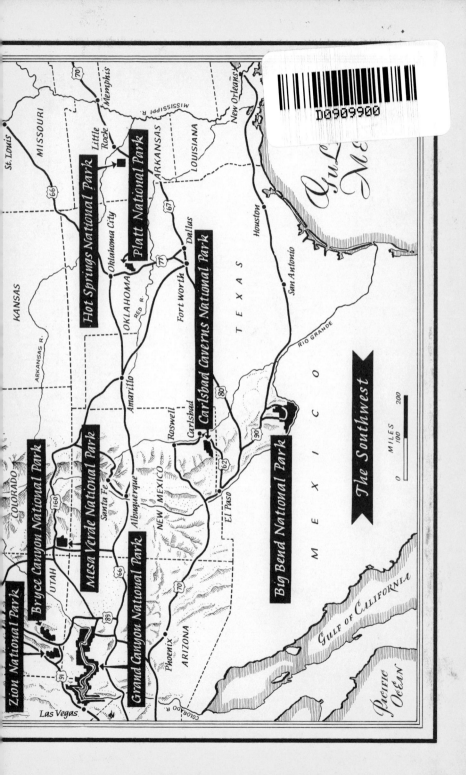

The REAL BOOK About
OUR NATIONAL PARKS

The REAL BOOK About
Our National
PARKS

By NELSON BEECHER KEYES

GARDEN CITY BOOKS

GARDEN CITY, NEW YORK

End papers and map opposite page 13 are by Rafael Palacios

TO CHRIS AND AMY

With love, and the hope that they, too, will be proud of that great heritage which is their native land

ACKNOWLEDGMENTS

THE AUTHOR wishes to offer his grateful thanks to Mr. Ralph Anderson of the Bureau of Information, and to the many other kind ladies and gentlemen of the Washington office of the National Park Service, for their generous aid and many kindnesses in connection with the preparation of this book. He also feels a deep and lasting debt of gratitude to a host of superintendents, rangers, naturalists, and other members of the field forces of this very admirable branch of our federal government for their assistance and many attentions during his visits to so many of our wonderful national parks over the years.

CONTENTS

Our Wonderful National Parks   13

The Men and Women of the National Park Service   18

Things to Know about the National Park Service   23

Yellowstone   30

Yosemite   36

Sequoia—Kings Canyon   42

Mount Rainier   48

Crater Lake   54

Wind Cave   60

Mesa Verde   66

Platt   72

Glacier   77

Rocky Mountain   84

Hawaii   90

Lassen Volcanic   97

Mount McKinley   104

Acadia   111

Grand Canyon   117

Zion   124

Hot Springs   130

Bryce Canyon   136

Grand Teton   142

Great Smoky Mountains   149

Carlsbad Caverns   156

Shenandoah   163

Mammoth Cave   169

Olympic   175

Isle Royale   182

Big Bend   189

Everglades   196

Virgin Islands   202

These Other National Areas Deserve Your Attention   209

Index   213

ILLUSTRATIONS

SUBJECT	BETWEEN PAGES	SUBJECT	BETWEEN PAGES
Badger Pass Ski Lift	30–31	Mount McKinley	94–95
Beach Scene, Virgin Islands	190–191	Mount Rainier	30–31
Bryce Canyon	126–127	Nisqually Glacier, Rainier	30–31
Cave Island Falls	30–31	Old Faithful, Yellowstone	30–31
Cliff Palace, Mesa Verde	62–63	Ouachita Mountain Country	126–127
Crater Lake	30–31	Overlook, Great Smoky Mountains	158–159
Duncan Bay, Isle Royale	190–191	Rock of Ages, Carlsbad	158–159
Frenchman Bay	126–127	Santa Elena Canyon	190–191
Frozen Niagara, Mammoth Cave	158–159	Skyline, Shenandoah	158–159
Giant Sequoia Trees	30–31	Snow Ball Dining Room	158–159
Grand Canyon, Air View	94–95	Temple of the Sun	158–159
Grand Canyon, South Rim	94–95	Three Patriarchs, Zion	126–127
Grand Teton Range	158–159	Trail into Grand Canyon	94–95
Great White Throne, Zion	126–127	Trail Scene, Rocky Mountain	62–63
Grinnell Glacier	62–63	Tree Ferns, Hawaii	94–95
Kings River Canyon	30–31	Wind Cave	30–31
Lake McDonald	62–63	Woodland Trail, Isle Royale	190–191
Loch Vale, Rocky Mountain	62–63	Yellowstone Falls	30–31
Mammoth Hot Springs	30–31	Yosemite Valley	30–31
Mount Lassen	94–95		

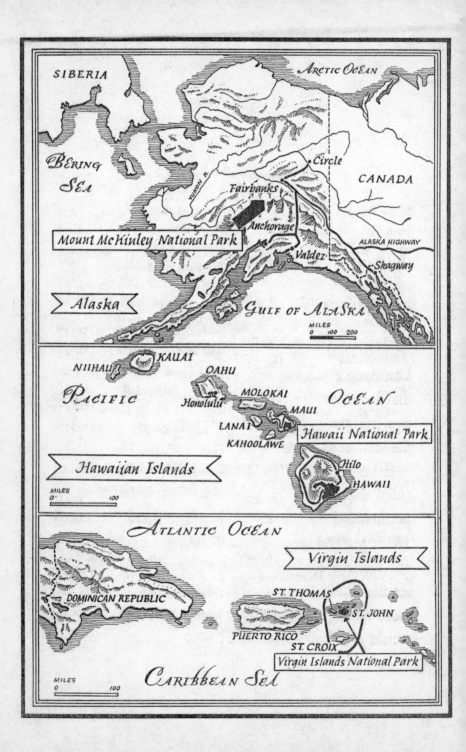

OUR WONDERFUL
NATIONAL PARKS

WHILE it may not seem possible today, there was a period in the early 1800s when many thinking people believed that much of the mighty stretch west of the Mississippi River was nothing but a vast "American desert." Jefferson, at the time he made the Louisiana Purchase, felt certain we would draw upon that huge territory very slowly, and it might be a full two hundred years before some parts of it admitted the first settlers.

Even before Arkansas was named, it had been decided that a part of this region would become the permanent home of the Indians. Fort Smith, erected in 1817, marked what was then thought would long be our western frontier. In those days it may well have seemed that as a nation we were land-poor, and had more natural wonders and dazzling scenery than we would ever know what to do with.

Yet it was in this very same Arkansas area that our national park system had its beginning, and only fifteen years after Fort Smith was founded. There, in 1832, a group of warm springs with seemingly magical healing powers that gushed from the foot of a wooded hill in the Ouachita Mountains, together with four square miles of surrounding land, were set aside as the Hot Springs Reservation. It would be many years before the preserve was raised to park status, but here was the pattern for a program that became active almost a half century later.

By then the United States extended to the Pacific Ocean and beyond. Great sections of what had once been judged worthless land were now being opened to settlement and other uses. Some of them, such as the great forest areas, were being stripped of their ageless beauty. Certain farsighted men, however, began to realize that there were natural wonders, such as the Hot Springs, which could be misused under private ownership, or defaced, and their loveliness or other appeal lost forever. All such should be set apart as reservations so that their unique qualities might be *conserved*, and kept for the benefit of all the people throughout all time.

When the Department of the Interior was organized

in 1849, its purpose was to manage, conserve, and develop our natural resources. One of its chief interests was "to prevent waste." And so it was that when some of America's wonderlands seemed to be threatened, and might very well be laid waste, it was decided that especially deserving areas were to be set aside. But all such were to be unique. In some manner they must be singular, peculiar, and without like or equal.

Starting in the early 1870s, possible candidates began to come up for consideration. Yellowstone, with its unsurpassed geyser display, was one. Yosemite, with its glacier-carved valley and plumelike waterfalls, another. And, as the years crept by, there were other tracts, many with the most noble and inspiring scenery, such as the breath-taking group of mountains in northwestern Montana, or the immense, yawning, vivid canyon bulldozed through the high mesa country of Arizona by the restless Colorado River. These points of scenic splendor, together with others having some outstanding or unusual quality, deserved to be properly guarded and administered, since they are "supreme examples" of the splendor and grandeur of our country.

There was a tendency at first to lock them away. But even though museum pieces require safekeeping, they still merit being seen by the greatest possible num-

15

ber. And our excellent National Park Service, established in 1916, is doing its best today to encourage all Americans to visit, enjoy, and profit by the marvels which it administers in the public interest. Its duty and purpose is to "conserve the scenery, and the natural and historic objects, and the wildlife" in the areas within the system, "and to provide for the enjoyment of the same in such manner and by such means as will leave them unimpaired for the enjoyment of future generations." One other of its tasks is to determine that all new areas brought to park status are worthy, and are indeed *supreme* examples of their kind.

They must be of a quality with Mount Rainier, which has the finest single-peak glacier system in the world. Or with Crater Lake, one of the deepest, bluest, and most handsome of all bodies of water. All candidates must be of a kind with Mount McKinley, loftiest peak above its base the world around, or Hawaii, with its largest living volcano, or Sequoia, in which grow the big trees, earth's oldest growing things. Thus they are superb specimens—even the very newest among them, that rare and remarkable tropical jewel in the Virgin Islands, just made the twenty-ninth member of this select company.

And because they are such carefully chosen wonder-lands, they now draw close to 50,000,000 visitors each year. So may the brief visits to each of them made in following pages encourage countless others to join this mighty throng. They are presented in this book in the order in which they were established as parks.

THE MEN AND WOMEN OF
THE NATIONAL PARK SERVICE

BESIDE the 29 national parks, the National Park
Service administers 12 other types of areas, or
more than 180 pieces of property in all. These embrace
those places which have our most inspiring scenery,
or are in some manner of outstanding historic, prehistoric, or scientific interest. They are federal areas, and
thus separate and distinct from state and local parks
and preserves. More than 80 of the above total are
national monuments, which are areas like the parks
but not as unusual, not quite such unique examples of
beauty or wonder. In most instances, too, they are more
limited in size.

Beyond the national parks and monuments there
are the battlefield, historical, memorial, and military
parks; battlefield and historic sites; monuments, memorials, cemeteries, parkways, recreation areas, and
the National Capital Parks, which comprise 790 units

located in the District of Columbia, Virginia, Maryland, and West Virginia. The Service is responsible for managing, guarding, patrolling, and, in most cases, maintaining more than 24 million acres of federally owned land, and about three quarters of a million privately owned acres within the boundaries of these national preserves. It is a huge and complicated task, and calls for the faithful, dedicated service of many capable people. Fortunately, able leadership has always attracted just such into this interesting work.

Some of them are women. There are nurses in attendance at many of the more than 180 administered areas, and some of them are National Park Service employees. A far greater number serve as secretaries, typists, and office workers in national or regional headquarters, and in the larger field offices.

But by far the greater number of Park Service personnel are men. Some wear the well-known, attractive green uniform with the stiff-brimmed Stetson hat. But many do not, for there are numerous jobs to be done, and a need for truck drivers, telephone linemen, historians, archaeologists, caretakers, and a score or more of other classes of work. Best known to the visitors are the park rangers, park naturalists, ranger naturalists, and tour leaders. It is their duty to meet the public and help it to enjoy, understand, and appreciate the parks and other federal areas.

The duties of the park ranger may involve any or all of the following: protection of forests from fire, as well as protection of scenic areas and their plants, trees, and wildlife. He may have to plant young fish in lakes and streams, give information to the public, and keep park visitors from harm to themselves or to the public domain. He is called upon, of course, to preserve law and order, to prevent accidents, and to register visitors. In some parks he may collect fees and issue automobile use permits or grant admittance when such charges are made. Rangers are in charge of assigned areas of a park or monument, or of certain portions of the work in a ranger district. Not a few of them serve as engineers, architects, and landscape architects. Some are college trained, but that is not necessary, for all must take examinations for entrance into the Service.

Park naturalists are permanent employees, while ranger naturalists work only at those seasons when the number of visitors is largest. But in either event their duties may include any of the following tasks. They often lead groups on field trips, explaining points of interest, and tell about the birds, flowers, plants, trees, wildlife, and the rocks and earth formation of the region. They often give talks on these subjects before tours start, or at evening campfires and other similar occasions. They may operate an information bureau, where they must be prepared to answer questions on each and every subject relating to the region they serve. Or they may work in a museum, contacting the visitors, or collecting and preparing objects for display. While rangers and naturalists lead parties on trips of various sorts, there are certain parks in which there are regular tour leaders, as in the case of the three which have caverns and underground wonders. It is their duty to conduct visitors through certain areas, explaining all their features and giving talks and lectures as may be necessary. Since they are skilled in such work, they help add much to the visitors' enjoyment.

There is a real touch of romance to the work in the National Park Service. The men who join its ranks as rangers and in other jobs like their work, and stay on year after year. This means that there are not too many openings for new men. As a consequence the Service can pick the very best of those seeking to become members. Still it is always glad to hear from those who might care to wear its uniform, or join its loyal forces. Here is what, in spirit, those who are accepted promise in connection with their jobs.

We as members of the Civil Service accept our obligation and our opportunity to serve the American people well and in full measure, doing our best to further the free and democratic institutions of our country.

We believe it is our duty to . . . .

Carry out loyally the will of the people as expressed in the laws . . . .

Serve the public with fairness, courtesy, integrity, and understanding . . . .

Help improve the efficiency, economy, and effectiveness of our work . . . .

And thus do our part in performing the great services of government.

THINGS TO KNOW ABOUT THE
NATIONAL PARK SERVICE

VISITORS to our national parks not only ask many questions about the particular park they are visiting, but they ask many other questions, too. These have to do with all the parks and the fine Service which administers them for the enjoyment of millions of our people each year. Here are some of the questions most often asked, and brief answers to each of them.

Do other nations have national parks? Yes indeed. Canada has about the same number that we have. Mexico, our other next-door neighbor, has several; and so do 20 other nations.

Who makes the regulations and rules for the parks? They are made occasionally by Congress, and more often by the Secretary of the Interior, or the Director of the National Park Service. They are merely to carry out the laws, or to protect the visitors, or park property;

and each rule or regulation has a good, sound reason behind it.

How do the parks differ from one another? Although some parks may seem to be very similar, as for instance the three which feature caverns, a visit to them will show that their underground wonders are actually decidedly different. Some parks are scenic, while others are volcanic. One produces warm water with curative powers, while the mineral springs in another flow cold water. So different are they, in fact, that it is rather hard to assign them to clear-cut classifications.

Are new areas being added to the Park System? Usually quite a number of areas are proposed as new parks each year, but almost all of them fail to qualify. They either are not of sufficient *national* importance, or are not amply outstanding. Once in a great while an area is demoted from park status because another area of the same type proves more deserving.

How are national parks established? A national park is set up only by act of Congress after much research and investigation by the Park Service. A national monument requires only presidential proclamation; and several parks were formerly monuments.

What is the difference between parks and monuments? National monuments are usually outstanding examples of historic, prehistoric, scientific, or scenic excellence. The park is a step higher, and is a *superior and unsurpassed example.*

What difference is there between national parks and national forests? Usually national parks are scenic areas or wonderland types that are unique, and cannot be replaced in like kind. Forests, by contrast, are primarily timber-growth areas, set aside so they may develop naturally, together with their wildlife and other features. National forests are administered by the Forest Service, a division of the Department of Agriculture.

How do park and recreational areas differ? A park is established to protect and safeguard areas which can be enjoyed best in their most natural state. The other type of area is managed and developed chiefly so that the greatest number may find recreational enjoyment within its bounds. Hunting, which is forbidden in all national parks, may well be permitted in recreational areas. The rules governing their use are usually much less strict.

How many people work for the Park Service? There are about 3600 men and women who are employed full time. Most parks have their greatest number of visitors in the summer, while two or three are busiest during the winter months. Normally there are some 3000 additional seasonal employees hired on a part-time basis to help during these peak periods.

Does the Park Service operate hotels, lodges, camps, stores, and similar facilities within parks? In all areas where facilities for visitor comfort and enjoyment are necessary, they are operated by private companies or individuals, called *concessionaires,* and not by the Park Service or by the federal government. These services are carried on under a contract or permit, and charges made for them are always approved by the National Park Service. Long experience has proved that the public is best served by this method of operation.

Why are fees charged in some of the parks? Such fees as are charged are in accord with policies established by Congress. Most parks have fees for the use of motor vehicles within their boundaries, and the amount of the fee varies with the benefits enjoyed by the visitors. In some cases there are no charges, since for sufficient reasons they are not justified. In a few parks there are admittance or tour fees where visitors need to be accompanied by a guide. The money so paid in actually amounts to less than one fourth the total cost of park operation.

Why are there not more roads in some of the parks? Roads are built only after it is certain they will not upset natural conditions within the park. Sometimes a road with its frequent traffic may exert strange and even unfortunate influences upon wildlife and other park features. Also since roads must be built and maintained from funds provided by Congress, there is often not enough money on hand to meet the very high cost of constructing highways through rugged, remote areas.

Why is wildlife abundant in some parks and very limited in others? In two of our parks, Hawaii and Virgin Islands, wildlife is highly limited in all surrounding territory as well. In certain others, the natural food supply is too limited for animals ever to increase within the park limits. On the other hand, there are some areas in which the animals do increase faster than their food supply, and carefully calculated numbers are killed each year, rather than let them starve.

Why can you fish—but not hunt—in the parks? Fish multiply so much faster than land animals that there is little trouble keeping streams and lakes suitably stocked. Even with strictly regulated hunting, many animals would vanish in a few seasons if hunted.

Why are there no golf courses, baseball diamonds, tennis courts, and such facilities in our parks, as there are in Canadian national parks? The parks in the United States were established so that the greatest possible number might find enjoyment from "scenery, the natural and historic objects, and the wildlife." It was felt that recreational needs are suitably served in town and city parks and playgrounds. While skiing and certain other winter sports have been encouraged in some parks, these are activities which demand considerable space, and require slopes or cross-country trails not elsewhere so well provided.

What do park employees do in the winter time? Since the needs of visitors must be the chief concern of most park employees, many tasks have to be set aside during part of the year. Also after an active season, equipment has to be repaired and facilities rebuilt or extended. There are reports to be made out and many preparations completed for the season ahead. Wildlife may need attention, too, in preparation for winter. And once the snows begin, which may be as early as late October in some areas, there are snow removal and other strenuous chores to care for during the cold months, when temperatures in some parks may drop to 30°, 40°, or even 50° below zero at times. Then, too, there is another visitor season not too far ahead, after the snow has melted and the spring flowers are in bloom—and it must be prepared for. The bears, the marmots, and certain park animals can hibernate, but not the rangers and other park employees. Winter usually is a very busy season for them.

YELLOWSTONE

THE RETURN of Lewis and Clark from their trip to the Pacific strengthened the belief that the country beyond the Missouri was not fit for white habitation or use. The following year, 1807, one of the expedition's former members was busy prospecting for beaver and other fur-bearing creatures. This rugged, hardheaded mountain man, John Colter, worked his way into the high plateau country in what is now northwestern Wyoming. His eyes could hardly believe what they saw there. But he later carefully described the improbable wonders he had discovered, and people promptly began to call the area "Colter's Hell." To men looking for more and better farming country, here was further evidence the "West" was well-nigh worthless.

Some years later, another mountain man made a trip into this almost unbelievable section. He was Jim

Photo by Northern Pacific Railway

Above: Strikingly colored hot springs and other hot-water phenomena occur at many points in Yellowstone. This new set of terraces at Mammoth is easily reached by auto.   *Below left:* A few of the park's many geysers, like Old Faithful, erupt at regular intervals.   *Below right:* Lovely Lower Falls is easily photographed from points on Yellowstone's Grand Canyon.

Western Ways Photo   *Photo by Northern Pacific Railway*

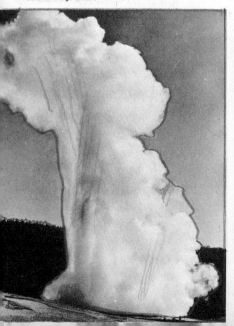

Above: Looking east into majestic Yosemite Valley from the portal of Wawona Highway tunnel. El Capitan is at the left, Half Dome is in the distance, and Bridalveil to the right. *Below left:* This pair of giant trees dwarfs visitors to the groves in Sequoia National Park. *Below right:* Nature in the raw very aptly describes this view in Kings Canyon National Park.

Above: Mount Rainier rears its massive summit high above these riders on Tatoosh Trail. The view is north over Paradise Valley, one of the park's recreational areas. *Below left:* Badger Pass ski lift in Yosemite, typical of fine facilities in many of the parks. *Below right:* Looking out onto Nisqually Glacier, one of Mount Rainier's twenty-six active ice rivers.

Above: Peaceful, inspiring Crater Lake has very blue water, is surrounded by high cliffs. Wizard Island in the foreground is the remains of a tiny extinct volcanic cone.   *Below left:* Wind Cave is famous for its beautiful boxwork ornaments, rather than massiveness.   *Below right:* Platt's lively streams and wooded hills are much appreciated in prairie country.

Bridger, equally hard of head, but he had a clever way with words. The stories told about steam jets, mud volcanoes, boiling water springs, and other seemingly impossible objects quickly whetted people's curiosity and also secured Jim's reputation as a teller of tall tales.

However, it was years later, when the railroad had pushed west and more and more people had had a look at this wonderland, that there came the feeling it should be kept unspoiled for all time. So it was that in 1872 it was set apart as our first national park, and its more than 2,000,000 acres make it still our largest. It is roughly a rectangle, about 62 miles from north to south, and averaging 54 miles wide. More than 90 per cent of its area lies in Wyoming, while a very small part is in Montana, and a trace in Idaho.

The central portion of the park is a high plateau, averaging about 8000 feet. Except to the southwest, this rolling tableland is surrounded by great, snow-capped mountains, which rise an added 2000 to 4000 feet. Both flatlands and peaks are volcanic in origin, and the region is now in the final, non-violent stages of volcanic action. Consequently the chief scenic features of the park are the geysers and the many other thermal, or hot water, wonders.

There are seven principal geyser basins—Norris,

Lower, Midway, Upper, West Thumb, Heart Lake, and Shoshone, which lie principally in the west and south-central parts of the park. The many, many geysers in these various sections are quite different in size, type, character, and action. Some few of them, such as Old Faithful, Riverside, and Daisy erupt their columns of steam and hot water at quite regular intervals. Others are exceedingly irregular. Some shoot upwards to great heights, while many send out tiny streams, or merely bubble, foam, or snort when erupting. The walls of the cracks or tubes of the geysers are formed of deposits of silica, which makes them strong enough so they may function properly. That is why the geysers are found principally in areas where this stronger rock is present.

Along with them there are marvelously colored hot springs, mud volcanoes, fumaroles, and other very strange formations. Outstanding are the Mammoth Hot Springs at the extreme north of the park, with others near Norris and West Thumb. These carry immense quantities of a white mineral in solution, and build up high terraces on which are very beautiful encrusted basins big enough in some instances to cover trees about and over which they have formed. Microscopic plants growing in some of the springs color the basins pink, red, or bluish gray, while the water in certain deeper pools is intensely green.

Several large rivers, such as the Yellowstone, Snake, Shoshone, Madison, and Lewis have their sources in this height of land whose waters divide between the Atlantic and the Pacific. The Yellowstone River has cut a grand canyon in the north-central part of the park, which is 2000 feet deep in places. Its walls are very colorful, ranging through oyster white, pale lemon, orange, pink, and crimson, along with the deep green of the forest cover. Its lower falls are 308 feet, or nearly twice as high as Niagara, while the upper falls roar down 109 feet. Other falls that can also be seen from an automobile include Lewis, Moose, and Gibbon.

Yellowstone makes up one of the largest wildlife sanctuaries in the whole world. For several generations the creatures have had full protection, and the animals no longer fear man. In fact, it has become necessary to keep visitors away from the bears, who are likely to bestow painful tusk and claw marks when food is not forthcoming promptly enough or in sufficient quantity. There are brown, black, and cinnamon bears, even some grizzlies, but they are not to be trusted. Those visitors who get out onto the trails away from the motor roads are quite likely to find herds of mule deer, wapiti, or elk, pronghorn antelope, bighorn mountain sheep, moose, and buffalo. There are many smaller creatures beside, and some 200 species of birds. About the several large lakes there are fish-eating ospreys, gulls, pelicans, ducks, and geese, while eagles hover over the higher crags. Both the lakes and flowing streams abound with trout.

Those who go to Yellowstone by train arrive either at the North Entrance at Gardiner, or at Yellowstone, at the West Entrance, both in Montana. There is, of course, access for busses and private cars at these two points, as well as at the Northeast Entrance at Silver Gate, the East Entrance convenient to Cody, Wyoming, and the South Entrance which connects with Grand Teton National Park only a few miles down the Snake River to the south. A very great share of the park's wonders can be seen from the more than 240 miles of pavement within its limits. There is also an extensive series of foot and pack trails.

The main season is from about June 20 to September 10. At that time the hotels, lodges, shelter cabins, campgrounds and other accommodations and facilities are in full operation. While visitors are permitted at other times, they are not encouraged. During the open season naturalists conduct nature walks and campfire talks daily at several points. There are museums at Mammoth, Old Faithful, Norris, Madison Junction, Fishing Bridge, and Obsidian Cliff, which help to make the park more understandable.

By auto road Yellowstone is some 350 miles southeast of Glacier National Park, about 550 from Denver and 460 from Cheyenne. It is nearly 800 miles east of Seattle and close to 1000 from San Francisco, while Chicago lies almost 1400 miles farther east.

YOSEMITE

THOSE who swarmed into California in search of gold in 1849 soon discovered there were other quite wonderful things there as well. Only two years later a group of them in pursuit of Indians wandered into a valley in the high hills about 150 air miles due east of San Francisco that has few equals for beauty anywhere in the world. Soon there was interest enough in this area so that in 1864 Congress set aside the Yosemite Valley and the neighboring Mariposa Grove of big trees, and turned them over to the state of California to administer for all the people for all time. Later other surrounding areas were acquired and in 1890 became Yosemite National Park, of which the valley and the grove were made a part in 1906.

This mighty gorge 7 miles long, and averaging a mile in width and a half mile in depth, is easily the best-known feature within the 1200 square miles of park area. Pictures of Half Dome, the hooded monk in stone brooding over its eastern end, or El Capitan, the smoothed slab more than 3600 feet high that stands guard near the valley's entrance, or lovely, wispy, wind-blown Bridalveil Falls, and other startling features are known across the world. Countless ages ago the Merced River cut a narrow, V-shaped canyon, which the glaciers slowly broadened into a U-shaped trough. Then the river again took over, and built the meadowlands that now form the valley floor. Scattered across it are the park headquarters, Yosemite Village, and hotels, lodges, cabin camps, museums, and other facilities for its enjoyment by great numbers of visitors.

Toward its eastern end, Glacier Point rises more than 3200 feet, and on its summit is a hotel and a public campground from which there are beautiful views of the valley beneath, and of the High Sierras to the north and east. One of the popular summer features takes place each evening on this point. A great heap of burning brush is pushed over its edge to cascade down in a flaming fireball to a barren ledge some 900 feet below.

Outstanding among the park's other features are its waterfalls. In this respect, there is no other area of equal size in the world to compare with it. At the head of the list is Yosemite Falls. Its upper section plunges 1430 feet in one single, unbroken drop. It next dashes down a series of steep cascades, and then leaps another 320 feet, for a total fall of 2425 feet. Next highest is Ribbon, with a drop of 1612 feet, while others that have become famous include Bridalveil, 620; Nevada, 594; Illilouette, 370; and Vernal, 317. The falls begin to pick up in volume as the winter snows start to melt, and are at their best in May and June. They taper off during the summer, and in very dry years some do not flow between mid-August and the onset of the rainy season in November.

Many visitors swing off just inside the South Entrance and visit the Mariposa Grove of giant sequoias. There are thousands of younger trees and at least 200 patriarchs above 3000 years old. The monster tree among them is the Grizzly Giant, which began its life at about the time the Biblical twins Esau and Jacob were born, some 3800 years ago. Its girth is 96½ feet, its diameter 29½ feet, and it is 209 feet tall. Also in Mariposa is the Wawona tree, which has a roadway 26 feet long passing right through the trunk. There are two smaller groves in the park—the Merced and the Tuolumne.

Reached by road only at its eastern and western

ends is the highly scenic Tuolumne Basin. This includes the beautiful Hetch Hetchy Valley and Reservoir, the Grand Canyon of the Tuolumne, and Waterwheel Falls, in which great arcs of water are flung from 60 to 80 feet into the air. In its upper reaches is Tuolumne Meadows, the largest subalpine gardens in the High Sierra. Standing 8600 feet above sea level, this is an ideal starting point for many foot and horseback trips into a vast domain of granite peaks dotted with lakes and mountain meadows that make up the "High Country." Some 700 miles of trail radiate from Tuolumne Meadows and Yosemite Valley.

Altitude within the park ranges from about 2000 to over 13,000 feet. As a consequence there is a very wide variety of plant life, more than 1300 species of which are flowering types. There are some 60 species of mammals, the largest of which are the deer and the bears. Fawns are born during June and July, and can sometimes be seen with their mother does where the meadow grass is not too tall. In November the herds head for the lowlands to avoid Yosemite's deep snows. At that same time, the bears, marmots, beavers, and some other creatures go into hibernation, some of them for nearly seven months.

But while much of the park takes a long winter rest,

two of its four entrances are open all year. Badger Pass Ski Center, 20 miles by road from Yosemite Valley and at 7300 feet elevation, draws 100,000 winter-sports fans each year. There is a ski lodge, where equipment may be rented, and food and overnight accommodations may be had. A T-bar lift and rope tows are available at the runs; and a shelter hut is maintained nine miles over the trail at Ostrander Lake for experienced cross-country skiers. There is a skating rink and toboggan slide in Yosemite Valley, and the winter season lasts from mid-December to about March 1.

Summer, however, is the great season for visitors, and Arch Rock Entrance, a little over 60 miles from Merced via State Route 140, and South Entrance, about the same distance north of Fresno over State Route 41, are always open. Big Oak Flat Entrance, connecting with State Route 120 from the west, gives access to Tioga Road. This crosses the park to Tuolumne Meadows, and to Tioga Pass Entrance, where it continues on into Owens Valley to the east. This cross-park road was first an Indian trail and then a mine roadway before Yosemite became a park. But it climbs through high country, and can be used in summer only, especially the eastern portion.

Visitors may go as far as Merced or Fresno by railroad, plane, or through busses. There is local bus service into the park daily throughout the year from Merced, and daily during the summer from Fresno. There are many fine places to stay—hotels, lodges, housekeeping cabins, and even housekeeping tents. Other tent camps will be found along the lovely High Sierra Trail, with campgrounds throughout the park. There are also guided tours, museums, exhibits, and campfire talks to make visits much more worthwhile.

SEQUOIA–KINGS CANYON

MILLIONS upon millions of years ago, when mammoths and dinosaurs roamed the earth, they may very well have taken shelter in the groves of big trees that were then spread pretty generally across the world. But today these largest of all growing things are found only in a narrow belt about 250 miles long on the western slope of the Sierra Nevada, at elevations from 4000 to 8000 feet. They are towering evergreens, with huge, columnlike trunks, and are known as the *Sequoia gigantea.* They were named for the Cherokee silversmith, Se-quo-yah, who perfected an 86-character alphabet by which his tribesmen learned to read and write.

One day in the year 1858 Hale Tharp, a pioneer cowman at Three Rivers in east-central California, was led some 20-odd miles up into the hills over an ancient trail by friendly Indians. At last they passed the foot of Moro Rock and were soon in the Giant Forest. Thus Tharp became the first white man to see the fabulous big trees that grow so profusely in this area.

Others came to know and love these age-old patriots, and began to demand that the many groves of them in Tulare County be set aside. But it was not until the logging industry was making considerable inroads that Congress established Sequoia National Park in September 1890. A few days later it set up General Grant National Park, which included other fine groves of big trees but a few miles distant. North of these two preserves, and also in the very heart of the lofty Sierra, lay a wild mountain area through which the South Fork of the Kings River had slashed a rugged canyon. This newer section was eventually combined with the now discontinued General Grant Park to form a new Kings Canyon National Park in 1940. Although established separately, Sequoia and Kings Canyon are operated as though but a single park.

Within their more than 1300 square miles are towering mountains, deep canyons, magnificent forests. Despite the fact that Mount Whitney, at the extreme eastern edge of the park, is the highest point in the continental United States, and there are numerous other peaks from 11,000 to more than 14,000 feet, it is without doubt the forest patriarchs that give special distinction to the joint parks. Surely far more than half of all the big trees are found within their combined borders. Probably the finest stand of these largest and oldest living things is Giant Forest, about 17 miles in from the Ash Mountain Entrance. Here is found the herculean General Sherman Tree. Its height is 272 feet, while it is 101½ feet about the base. Thus it is 36½ feet through, or more than the width of many city streets. Even at 120 feet above the ground the trunk is still 17 feet in diameter. Ten feet higher up is the tree's largest branch, nearly 7 feet thick.

While this is the king of kings, it has a number of close rivals—in fact, scores of others almost as large are found in the various groves throughout the two parks. These big trees seem to prefer to grow in groups, rather than singly, and it is a thrilling experience to walk among them, and to realize what stalwarts they are. They have stood there between 3000 and 4000 years, have survived the ravages of countless fires, have the power of healing their deep scars, and each year produce thousands of tiny cones, from which new seedlings grow. Even the remains of the trees cut years ago for timber are impressive, as their ghostly reminders at Big Stump Basin, Redwood Mountain, and Converse Basin will show.

But even the huge sequoias tend to lose their size and thrill as the view is directed across Kern Canyon to Mounts Whitney, Langley, Barnard, and the other mighty mountains to the east, or when it sweeps north and south over the High Country from Pavilion Dome to Coyote Peaks. While the big trees can be found and seen from the auto roads, here are features that challenge the hardier types to take to the hills. Many fit packs to their backs and set off over the foot trails in search of adventure. Some carry recommended equipment and make successful climbs of certain of the jagged, and demanding peaks, for the Sequoia-Kings Canyon country offers fine opportunities for mountaineering. Since there are extensive numbers of saddle horses and pack mules that can be rented, many enjoy pack trips, ranging all the way from single-day jaunts to points of special interest up to trips of a week or more with competent guides into the High Sierra. Such saddle journeys may begin at the renting corrals at Giant Forest, Wolverton, General Grant Grove, or Cedar Grove in mile-deep Kings Canyon. There are numerous campgrounds in the Giant Forest and General Grant Grove areas, and four large ones about the ranger station in the Cedar Grove area. This latter is thus a popular basing point for longer trail trips.

Among the larger animals, the most generally seen in the parks is the mule deer, quite common and tame. There are numerous bears, and squirrels are everywhere, but the other animals keep pretty much out of sight. Birds are many and varied, and even golden eagles can often be seen wheeling above the higher crags. Among growing things other than the big trees, there are several other types of evergreens, some of which are very large examples of their species, and also a few hardwood trees, so that there is fall color, while in spring the lower country is brilliant with flowers.

While most visitors come to the parks in the summertime, there is skiing over a variety of runs at Wolverton, near Giant Forest. There is both skiing and tobogganing at Big Stump Basin near General Grant Grove, and a skating rink at Lodgepole. Skates, skis, and other equipment can be rented at these several points.

The two entrances are on the west side. That at Big Stump is reached from Fresno by State Route 180, and from Visalia by State Route 65, being a little over 50 miles from either city. Ash Mountain Entrance to

Sequoia is about 30 miles via State Route 198 from Visalia; and it is about 260 miles to San Francisco, and 225 to Los Angeles. The two entrances are open all the year, but are cut off from one another during the winter by snow.

There are lodges at both Giant Forest and General Grant Grove open in the summer, and the housekeeping cabins at the former are available through the winter, too. Even the coffee shop there never closes, while other eating places, stores, and facilities terminate their services in October, when the snows start. Some years this white blanket lies 12 to 16 feet deep. Most travel to Sequoia and Kings Canyon National Parks is by private car, although there are railroad, air-line, and bus-line services to Fresno or Visalia, and regular local bus service to General Grant Grove or Giant Forest during the summer.

MOUNT RAINIER

AMERICA'S highest and grandest volcano would hardly be taken for one on first sight. Yet such was the origin of Mount Rainier to the southeast of Puget Sound in the state of Washington. Long after a great reef of sandstone and shale rocks had been thrust up to form the Cascade Range, lava began to flow through fissures in the earth and in some places erupt and form mighty cones. It is around such volcanic action that four of our parks along the Pacific side of the Rocky Mountains—Yellowstone, Rainier, Crater, and Lassen—came into being.

Mount Rainier began with huge flows of a dark lava that still makes up its base. Then ashes and cinders were hurled out, more lava, and finally the cone tapered off in volcanic ash. The summit has been softened and rounded slightly, for it seems to be made up of two craters, one about a mile square, with a smaller one within. While a few small steam vents may still be found in the basin of the crater, a last bit of evidence that this is a volcano fast asleep, the enormous pile of earth, standing nearly two miles above its surroundings, is shrouded in snow and ice well down its flanks the year round.

At one time in the not too distant past, glaciers covered not only the mountain but much of the area down into Puget Sound. These heavily sculptured the mountain, leaving cirques, or large, rounded, steep-sided heads of valleys, and broad-floored, steep-walled canyons. No less than 26 active glaciers are still at work, wearing down Rainier. They grow slowly smaller, and are but remnants of what they once were, yet they run from 50 to 500 feet thick, and continue to cover more than 40 square miles of the mountainside. Nearly half of them are major exhibits, and some run from 4 to 6 miles, and their beauty rivals many found in the Alps.

Largest of the group is the Emmons Glacier, which is also the largest in the United States, flowing down from the summit to the northeast. It and the Nisqually on the south are most easily reached, and so the best known. The body of the latter near the center of its ice mass is moving just under a foot a day, or about 25 feet a month. At the present time the glaciers are melting slightly faster than the ice forms. Thus they are growing shorter. It has been figured that Emmons and Nisqually have each lost an average of 75 feet yearly during the last 20 years.

With its heavy cap of ice, the mountain is a breath-taking sight on clear days, when it can be seen for distances up to 150 miles. Consequently it was no secret to early explorers and settlers, yet it was not successfully climbed until 1870. But its great unique beauty was long fully appreciated, and in 1899 some 377 square miles with the mountain at its center were set aside as Mount Rainier National Park. And its setting is very much in keeping with the mountain itself.

The lower slopes of the mountain are covered by lush forests, including some trees of very unusual size. This forest cover reaches to about 7000 feet, above which are extensive flower gardens, their blooms thriving close beside the ice rivers. Indeed the park is famous for the very great beauty of its floral display. It is claimed that probably no area excels that of the park in abundance of bloom, or in the kinds of flowers represented. This display spreads through the various sections from May to September. The velvet-green beauty of the lowland forest is due to the abundance of rainfall, which amounts to about 9 feet a year. Much of this falls as snow, and during the colder months the views of the mountain are often shut off by storm clouds and fog. Warm, clear weather may be expected in the park from early July well into September, with a touch of Indian summer in October.

There are some 80 miles of pavement within the park that permit driving to many fine scenic points. In addition there are some 282 miles of trails to take hikers and horseback riders into all parts of the preserve, and even to the summit of Rainier. This latter is a difficult climb over ice fields, glaciers, and long patches of treacherous lava and pumice. Those who attempt it are required to give evidence of ability and of suitable physical stamina. It takes the practiced mountaineer a full day and much of the night to make the round trip to the top. That is if a blizzard is not encountered. The climbing season is only from June to early October.

Less arduous is the 90-mile Wonderland Trail which completely encircles the waist of the mountain. It has shelters and campsites at 8- and 12-mile intervals along it, so it may be used for trips from a single day to a full week. There is also the shorter Northern Loop Trail near the north boundary of the park.

There are four entrances, near the four corners of the preserve. The distance to Tacoma is from 52 to 65 miles, depending upon the entrance used, while it is from 62 to 85 miles to Seattle. Portland, Oregon is 162 miles, and Spokane 304. The Carbon River Entrance at the northwest serves the trails and camp areas. Nisqually River Entrance at the southwest gives access to the west side of Rainier in summer as far as the foot of the Puyallup Glacier, but principally to Longmire and Paradise Valley in the south foothills. The former is the park headquarters, and both are resort centers, Ohanapecosh Hot Springs Entrance at the southeast is the trail and camp center in that section. It is connected with White River Entrance to the northeast by the Mather Memorial Parkway. This road is open north to Cayuse Pass only in summer, for 15 feet of snow in this latter area is average. White River gives admittance to the trails and camps to the east, and the resort area about Sunrise.

Lodges and overnight accommodations within the park are available only from late June through early September. There are no overnight accommodations during the winter. Yet there is a winter season, primarily for skiing, which usually begins by mid-December, with sufficient snow to carry well along into May.

Rope tows are operated during this period, and a snack bar, warming hut, and first-aid room are open at Paradise Lodge. The road into this point is kept plowed, and is usable except briefly after heavy falls or slides. So that skiers may reach runs in the eastern portions, the Mather Parkway is kept open south to Cayuse Pass. Other park roads are generally closed after the first snowfall and remain snowbound until June.

CRATER LAKE

I T IS hard to believe that volcanoes have been highly
active in this country, and that great sections of large
mountains have either blown away in violent eruptions
or sunk back into the earth in fairly recent times. Yet
10,000 feet of the top of former Mount Mazama, in
what is now southwestern Oregon, disappeared not
over 7000 years ago. This giant catastrophe seemingly
took place after the Indians had come to live in the
area, for they carefully kept away from the remnants
of the mountain forever afterward, since ancient tradi-
tions claimed it to be the battleground of the Great
Spirits.

Geologists maintain that a mighty 12,000-foot
cone had been built up by a series of eruptions at a
point along the Cascade Range at the edge of a great
lava plateau that extended into parts of Washington,
Oregon, Idaho, and California. In one violent out-

burst, some 10 cubic miles of pumice were hurled out and scattered over many square miles. Then great cracks formed in the flanks of the mountain and in the neighboring earth, and the whole top collapsed and was drawn back into spaces within emptied by the eruption.

What was left was an enormous hole in the earth about 6 miles in diameter, with cliffs which in some places now rise as much as 2000 feet above a lake of unforgettable blue water. Lava seems to have welled up in the throat of the volcano and formed the floor of this gigantic crater. At a few points, vents encouraged small cones to form, and their tips rise above the 2000 feet of water that now partially fills this immense depression, and forms particularly beautiful Crater Lake.

Since the Indians so greatly feared the area, they seem to have given the early settlers no word of this startling body of water. It was first discovered by white men in 1853, when a party of prospectors chanced upon it. During the next 30 years, it had very few visitors. Then, in 1885, it was seen by William Gladstone Steel. Struck by its beauty, he conceived the idea of having this great natural wonder preserved as a national park. During the next 17 years he gave large amounts of his time and energy to this purpose, and some 250 square miles were finally set aside and established as Crater Lake National Park in May 1902. Steel gave the remaining 32 years of his life to its development, serving as its second superintendent, and then as park commissioner.

The lake is, of course, the dominant feature within the preserve. Its earliest discoverers named it Deep Blue Lake, while a later group decided it should be called Lake Majesty. Certainly it is majestic as viewed from any point along the 20-mile rim that surrounds it. These massive ramparts of pearly gray, splashed at some points with vivid colors, rise sharply from the waters. They are striped and mottled, too, with patches of the dark green of evergreen trees. But it is the inky blue surface—20 square miles of it, and spread wide before the eyes—that commands attention. Every drop of it, so far as can be learned, is from rain or snowfall, which in the area averages 72 inches of water annually. About 50 feet of snow sifts down in a normal winter.

This body of water has no inlet and no outlet, at least none except what may seep away through sides and bottom. Yet the surface elevation does not vary more than two or three feet throughout the year, evidence that intake, seepage, and evaporation are closely in balance. The water is crystal clear and very deep. For some reason it absorbs the other colors but reflects all of the blues in sunlight. Thus it is very deep in hue, and very placid and serene, because of its high protecting walls.

Crater Lake is about 250 miles south of Portland and 440 north of San Francisco. Closest city to the park is Klamath Falls, about 46 miles from South Entrance, and a few miles farther from East Entrance. The West Entrance is 69 miles from Medford, on important U.S. 99, and the North Entrance connects with another north-south highway, U.S. 97. Air, rail, and bus lines reach Medford and Klamath Falls, from which there are stage connections to the park daily from mid-June to mid-September.

During that three-month period, there are lodge, cabin, and camping facilities at Rim Village, which is at 7100 feet elevation and 950 feet above the lake. There are also picnic and campgrounds there, and a switchback trail down the canyon wall to the boat landing. Three other public campgrounds will be found along entrance roads, at Lost Creek, Cold Springs, and Annie Spring.

Roads through entrances to the West and South are kept open throughout the year. Those from North and

East entrances, together with Rim Drive, are closed in late September and reopened about July 1, dependent somewhat upon snow conditions. Since snow is so abundant, skiing is particularly good, and many come to enjoy it. Two trails from park headquarters to Rim Village are maintained throughout the winter. While there are warming-room facilities at Rim Village, no overnight accommodations can be had in the park during the colder months. This is a winter wonderland indeed, for the snowy splendor at Crater is truly magnificent. The deep blue lake is still very much in evidence, to be contrasted with the white of the snow, for its waters never freeze.

In the warm months, much time can be well spent exploring Rim Drive. Observation points along it afford excellent views of the lake. Castle Crest provides a good place to see Wizard Island, a cinder cone that thrusts up more than 760 feet above the water. Kerr Notch is possibly the best spot from which to view the Phantom Ship, a 170-foot rock formation that looks like a vessel under full sail. Garfield Peak, the Watchman, and Cloudcap are all vantage points close by Rim Drive from which magnificent views may be had.

Mount Scott, beyond Cloudcap and along the eastern boundary, is the highest point within park limits, 8938 feet. There is a trail to the fire lookout at its summit. About 4 miles south of it, near Wheeler Creek, are needlelike spires of pumice, some of them about 200 feet high. There are more of these shafts and columns to be seen in Godfrey's Glen and in Sand Creek Canyon.

Although private boats are not permitted on the lake, there is a daily launch trip around its waters each morning, and other scheduled trips daily to the Phantom Ship and Wizard Island. These all leave from the wharf below Rim Village, where rowboats can also be rented. Fishing from the shore is permitted, although trolling is recommended for the rainbow trout and silverside salmon with which the waters are "planted."

With the exception of black-tailed deer and bears, few larger animals are frequently seen. There is a wide variety of birds, and cormorants and gulls are common about the lake. During July and August there are colorful displays of wildflowers along the roads and about Rim Village.

WIND CAVE

IN THE southwestern corner of South Dakota there is a picturesque, mountainous region called the Black Hills. Some 6000 square miles in extent, it is rich in minerals, particularly gold, in scenery and natural wonders, and in history and lore. In fact it was its gold that brought the area into great prominence, when the Sioux Indians sought to drive out the white men who had flocked into their cherished hills which had been given them as a reservation. The final outcome of this uprising was Custer's bloody defeat at the battle of the Little Bighorn.

Now it seems there was an ancient legend which claimed that the Four Winds were the true gods of the Plains Indians. The Sioux were certain that these winds made their home in the Black Hills. In fact what later came to be called Wind Cave might very well have been the abode of the sacred breezes, and one of the reasons why the Indians fought so hard for the area when the whites attempted to take it over.

This whole section is a huge dome-shaped uplift. Its rocks, laid down on the ocean bottom, were thrust upward ages ago and the younger layers worn away. Some of these strata were granite, which pushed their way into place as molten rock. Others were great beds of limestone, very surely laid down beneath the waters of some ancient sea, for there are sea shells still embedded in the solid rock.

When water contains carbonic acid, as most rain and natural surface waters do, it attacks and dissolves limestone. As the mass of rock settles and ages, cracks and fractures break it up into blocks of various sizes. Water then seeps into these tiny crevices, dissolves the neighboring stone, until very slowly caverns, or great hollows underground, are formed. Many such caves occur in the Pahasapa limestone of the Black Hills.

What is probably the largest, and surely the strangest, of them all was discovered by mere chance in 1881. Tom Bingham, one of the early pioneers, was deer hunting at a point about 45 or 50 miles from where today Wyoming, South Dakota, and Nebraska meet. Pressing through the brush, he suddenly heard and felt a great rushing of air. After a quick search, he soon found a hole about 10 inches in diameter from which quantities of cooler air were flowing. He had stumbled upon one of nature's greatest curiosities, and the only natural opening to an enormous underground cavern. Later a larger entrance was opened up nearby. But still the air poured out on some days, and surged in on others. What was the cause?

Wind Cave, as it came to be known, was carefully studied. This phenomenon of air rolling in and out seemed to be closely tied to what is called atmospheric pressure. When the barometer, and thus the pressure of the air, is falling, the cave releases air, which blows out in a strong current, like wind. By contrast, when the barometer is rising, and outside pressure increasing, an inbound wind starts to blow. It is interesting to stand at the cave entrance, wet a finger, and hold it up to determine in which direction the air is then moving.

So very unique was this cave that it was decided it should never be turned into a business venture, but should become the property of all the people for all time. As a consequence, early in 1903 Congress set it aside as the sixth of our national parks. Subsequently its above-ground area was extended until it now embraces an L-shaped block of about 43½ square miles.

Western Ways Photo

Above: Mesa Verde's Cliff Palace once had some 200 rooms and sheltered over 400 people. It was built of well-laid masonry, with a four-story tower and eight floor levels.   *Below*: While Glacier Park's Lake McDonald lacks the more rugged beauty of certain of its neighbors, it is truly a vacation wonderland and can provide a memorable holiday.

E. N. Harrison

Above: This view across little Loch Vale is very typical of the superb scenery in Rocky Mountain National Park. The peak in the background rises to nearly 13,000 feet. *Below left:* While much of Rocky Mountain National Park is rugged, some trails can be very inviting. *Below right:* Grinnell Glacier is but one of many which gave their name to Glacier National Park.

Many caves are famous for their stalactites, or icicle-like formations that build up when water seeps through the roof; and also for the cone-shaped stalagmites that rise from the floor. There are very few of these in Wind Cave, which is noted instead for its boxwork decorations on walls and ceiling, which result in traceries, carvings, and lacework of the most elaborate and surprising description. Delicate veins and interlacings of calcite deposited in crevices are left standing out in relief as the softer limestone between is leached away by seeping water. Other interesting features include frostwork, curtains and sheets of flowstone, crystal-lined cavities, and strange shapes, some of which suggest plants and animals. Many of the decorations are pure white, while some are combined with a very delicate pink background.

All trips through the cave must be made in the company of park rangers, and a journey into the Post Office, Model Room, Elks Room, Blue Grotto, Fairgrounds, Monte Cristo Palace, and Garden of Eden takes about 1½ hours. There are ten tours at hourly intervals during the summer, four each day during the spring and fall, while in the winter months arrangements must be made in advance with the superintendent. There is a difference in elevation between the entrance and the lowest point reached of 240 feet, and visitors are returned to the surface by elevator. The underground temperature is 47° at all times, and a sweater or jacket in summer feels good. All underground sections are electrically lighted, and there are stairs at many points where the footing would otherwise be too steep or insecure. About ten miles of its passages have been explored, although but a small portion of them may as yet be visited.

The 28,000 surrounding acres of range and forest land actually compete strongly for interest with the cave itself. From the motor road through the park it is possible to see deer, antelope, and occasionally at morning and evening the elusive elk. There are prairie-dog towns, where there is always something to watch, while the truly rewarding sight is a far larger animal. It is claimed that the herd of buffalo, or American bison, that roams the park is the largest on the continent. Excellent views of these creatures may be had from cars driving along the highway.

While a public campground and lunchroom are available during the warmer months, there are no lodges or cabins to be had within the park itself. Customary tourist accommodations can be found at Hot Springs, about 10 miles south of the park boundaries, where there are also rail, air, and bus connections.

The park is bordered by Custer State Park and Harney National Forest to the north and west. It is about 75 miles over Alt. U.S. 85 to Lead, home of the fabulous Homestake, America's largest producing gold mine. A few miles further on is Deadwood, a place with a turbulent past, and closely associated with such characters as Wild Bill Hickok, Calamity Jane, Deadwood Dick, and Jack McCall. This same highway passes Harney Peak, whose 7242 feet are supposed to be the highest point east of the Rockies. Also north of the park, about 55 miles via Custer and U.S. 16—the Needles Highway—is South Dakota's magnificent emblem of democracy, the Mount Rushmore National Memorial. Here a whole mountainside is given to busts of George Washington, Thomas Jefferson, Abraham Lincoln, and Theodore Roosevelt.

MESA VERDE

ONE December day in 1888 Richard Wetherill and Charlie Mason, ranchers far down in southwestern Colorado, were hunting strays in the cedar and piñon forests that carpeted the mesa country to the north and west of the Mancos River. It was a rugged area. Once it had been a high plain, but through countless ages spring floods had cut a series of sharp, deep canyons in it. The waters of many centuries had washed away the softer earth, leaving the harder rocks in huge blocks like enormous tables between the canyons. The Spanish word for table is *mesa,* and the largest of these blocks of tableland cut by the tributaries of the Mancos River was called Mesa Verde —or green table—for it was covered by stunted evergreen trees in a part of our land where trees are very scarce.

Suddenly the two men stopped short in their tracks.

Across the narrow canyon on whose rim they stood, and nestling in a mighty cleft formed by the overhanging rocks at the top of the wall, was a large group of stone buildings. It appeared to be a city, but what these two cattlemen had discovered was one of the most celebrated prehistoric ruins in North America. They promptly named their find the Cliff Palace.

Later other ruins, slightly smaller but equally important and interesting, were located close by. One, a three-story apartment house, is thought to have at one time given shelter to 300 people. It is known as Spruce Tree House. There was also Balcony House, Square Tower House, and, of special interest, the Sun Temple. Here, along with numerous other pueblo ruins in the vicinity, was evidence of a valiant attempt to achieve a civilization. These remains deserved to be preserved; and in 1906 Mesa Verde National Park was established, and now embraces more than 51,000 acres.

Fortunately these cliff dwellings were fairly well preserved, and many relics of the past have been recovered from them. After years of careful study, this is what seems to have taken place in the ages before white men came to settle in our Southwest. About the time of Christ, Indians, who were farmers rather than hunters, moved into the Mesa Verde region. For several hundred years they lived in small caves and underground houses on top of the mesas. Between the fifth and the eighth centuries they learned to make pottery and also to build houses, the latter still partly underground. Then during the next 400 years they ceased building their pit homes and began to construct pueblos, or common dwellings, where family groups seem to have lived in separate apartments. At first these multiple homes were placed upon the tops of the mesas. Then in the twelfth and thirteenth centuries the Indians made great progress and built the very large dwellings which have been found in the immense caverns in the upper canyon walls.

Largest of these was the Cliff Palace, some 300 feet long. It had more than 200 living rooms, and probably housed about 400 people. While this pueblo, or village, which is the meaning of this Spanish word, was a continuous structure, its considerable population did not live a common life as though it was one big family. Instead, these people seem to have been divided into a series of units, either families or clans. Each group, and there appear to have been 23 such units in the Cliff Palace, was separate and distinct from the others. Each had its living rooms and storehouses. But more remarkable still, each had its own kiva or ceremonial room, which was also probably a place of worship. These were underground rooms often hollowed out of the solid rock. Here family or clan councils were held, attended presumably only by the men, for it is certain that the religious fraternities at least permitted only men and boys to membership.

The Mesa Verde people seem to have been very religious, worshiping the sun as the father of all, while the earth was the mother, and through her bounties they had their food and other material blessings. Although they made much progress in a dozen centuries, life was still rather difficult even in their golden age which seems to have come to a climax during the 1200s. This was a dry country at best, and water had to be carefully conserved and every drop made to count. Game was very scarce, and hunting both difficult and not too rewarding. There were a few berries and nuts to be carefully sought out, and the Mancos River yielded limited numbers of fish. Yet by care and good management they were able to maintain themselves and make considerable progress. It is a great pity they never learned to put their thoughts and experiences into writing.

Nature, however, has a way of leaving quite interesting records. One method is by means of tree rings. These not only show the age of the tree of which they are a part, but by their width and fullness can tell whether the year they represent was wet or dry. Through the extensive studies of many men, we now know much about the rainfall in large sections of this country during hundreds upon hundreds of years. We can be quite certain that not only the year 1276 but also the twenty-three that immediately followed it were unusually dry throughout the Southwest. There was a 24-year drought, so severe that it may well have caused the people who lived in the pueblos on Mesa Verde, and in that whole area, to abandon the cliff houses they had so skillfully built, and wander off in search of homes elsewhere. While their villages in the canyon walls show many evidences of having been cleverly fortified, it seems more certain that excessive dryness and the threat of famine, rather than some plundering human enemy, drove these peaceful farmers from their fine stone apartment houses. There is every reason to believe that the Cliff Palace had been empty for as much as 600 years before that day when two men in search of their wandering cows chanced upon one of the great wonders of our land.

The park entrance is 40 miles west of Durango and

220 south of Grand Junction, in Colorado, while it is about 150 miles down to Gallup, or nearly 260 to Santa Fe, in New Mexico. It is some 20 miles from the entrance in to headquarters, where the museums, lodge, and other facilities are located on Chapin Mesa. This pavement runs to or close by all the more important exhibits. However, there is a series of pack trails winding through the canyons and across the mesas. These are rather strenuous for hikers, but horseback trips over them are enjoyed by many. A cook-guide accompanies each party, and all members are provided with a saddle horse, bed, canteen, slicker, and food. Trips of several days' duration can be arranged.

During the summer season from May 15 to October 15 there is not only a lodge, but de luxe and housekeeping cabins, furnished tents, and also a public campground available within the park. The museums are then open, and there are the guided trips and campfire talks that help to make the ruins so much easier to understand. During the winter there are no overnight accommodations, and access to some of the exhibits is closed off temporarily after heavy snows.

PLATT

DOWN in the rolling prairie lands in the Washita River country in southern Oklahoma are two pleasant creeks, one emptying into the other. Tradition has it that even in the long ago the stream banks each spring were filled with tepees. But the Indians did not flock there to enjoy the early flowers, or to try their hand at fishing. Instead they came to benefit by the mineral springs that gushed from the earth. Their waters were "good medicine," as hundreds of thousands of people in more recent years have learned.

When this section of our country was set aside as Indian Territory, and divided principally between the Five Civilized Tribes, the area containing the creeks and their mineral springs was almost at the center of the lands of the Chickasaw Nation, established in 1867. Gradually portions of the Indian Territory were opened up to settlement. As more and more came to

72

live there, the popularity of the springs grew. It was felt they should belong to all the people, so surrounding lands were purchased from their Indian owners, and the Sulphur Springs Reservation was set up in 1902. Then in 1906, about a year before Oklahoma became a state, the name of the reservation was changed to Platt National Park. It was so called in honor of Senator Orville Hitchcock Platt of Connecticut, who had performed outstanding services for the Indians.

The area needed to protect the springs was not large, but its gently rolling hills were in pleasant contrast to the great stretch of level plains which surround the 900 acres within park boundaries. The reservation lies along the southern edge of the city of Sulphur, and is made up of a large central block, with a long eastern, and a much shorter western, projection.

The former accommodates picturesque Travertine Creek, fed principally by two enormous springs from which flow more than 5 million gallons of fresh water each day. They bear the names Buffalo and Antelope, and it is claimed that they once drew great herds of these creatures from surrounding grazing lands to drink of their sparkling waters. But although these mighty springs generally provide well over 150,000 barrels per day, they have been known to fail in times of extreme drought. For a considerable distance the road winds along both sides of attractive Travertine Creek, and there is a picnic area on an island in the stream, and Cold Springs Campground lies along its banks.

In addition to the fresh-water springs, there are a considerable number that are classed as sulphur springs, and three in which the chemical content is chiefly bromide. All of them flow cold water, in contrast to the hot springs in the national park of that name in Arkansas. Among the best known are Pavilion Springs, Bromide Spring, and Medicine Spring.

The former is near the end of Travertine Creek, not far from where it empties into Rock Creek, which enters the park from the city of Sulphur to the north. Close by the junction of these two streams is Black Sulphur Spring, whose waters are heavy with sulphur. It is within sight of lovely Floral Park, by the main entrance, and its curative waters are dispensed in a small pavilion. Nearby is Hillside Springs, also of sulphur content. These flow out of a rock wall just below the headquarters building.

Further on to the south along Rock Creek stands Bromide Hill, a steep bluff, nicely wooded, with cliffs that rise sharply 140 feet above the creek bed. There is a very touching Indian legend that still haunts this sightly spot. It recounts how a small remnant of the once powerful Delaware tribe sought shelter among the Chickasaws. Its Chief, an old man, had no sons, but one very beautiful daughter, named Deerface. Two young braves of the tribe were much in love with her, but try as she would, she could not decide between them. Finally it was arranged that the young men would gallop their ponies across the top of Bromide Cliff, and jump their steeds to the creek so far below. He who survived this ordeal would not only marry Deerfoot, but also one day become the tribal chief.

So the day was set, and in the presence of Indians from miles around the two brave contestants thundered across the little mount and hurled their ponies into the air, only to be dashed to death. Heartbroken, Deerface sped to the edge of the cliff and leaped to her own doom.

It is said that those who search carefully will find a place on the rocks of the cliff where her likeness is imprinted for all times. Medicine Spring, which gushes out from the base of the bluff, may still contain the tears of the comely Deerface. And there are those who say that Bromide Spring, whose waters are served in a pavilion just across on the north bank of Rock

Creek, are mixed with tears of the old Chief, whose loss was also great.

Many find Platt's waters very beneficial, and come to drink of them regularly. There are three well-equipped campgrounds and numerous attractive picnic areas, some of which have fireplaces and tables. But there are no overnight accommodations within the park limits.

While it is open all year, summer is its principal season. Then the swimming and wading pools along Travertine Creek are exceedingly popular. Many, however, plan a visit in April when the redbud is in bloom, while others come in October to enjoy the fall colors.

Turner's Falls is an ancient Indian camp area not too far away in the scenic Arbuckle Mountains. Prices Falls, also in the heart of the Arbuckles, is worth a visit, as is the Devil's Den, a strange granite boulder formation, near Tishomingo on the shores of lovely Lake Texoma.

GLACIER

STRADDLING the Continental Divide in the Rocky Mountains of northwestern Montana is one of our most unusual parks. Not only has it towering, knife-edge mountains, 60 flashing glaciers, and some 200 gemlike lakes, but it has another quite different claim to fame. With adjoining Waterton Lakes National Park in Canada, it forms the Waterton-Glacier International Peace Park, a marvelous gesture of good will in the wonderful relations that have so long existed between our two neighboring lands.

Glacier National Park is a living, exciting example of what happens as mountains are thrust up, and then carved and formed by glacial ice, flowing water and nature's other tremendous forces. Here you can thrill over lofty peaks, where once mighty ice rivers ground out great cirques, or cupped-in basins, one, two, or three thousand feet deep, high on their flanks. Then the gnawing action of ice, hard-frozen snow, or leaping water slashed out hanging, pitching valleys, through which cascades hurry down to fill robin's-egg blue lakes that glisten in the cool sunlight. Perhaps nowhere else are there mountains carved quite like these. Nowhere else does flowing water or a shimmering lake's surface seem to have the same exciting charm. While today's glaciers are but badly shrunken reminders of the monsters that once clothed this land, they are still most impressive, especially if one takes to the park's 1000-mile trail system and gets really close to these slow-moving ice rivers.

Although a portion of the park was included in a grant to Hudson's Bay Company in 1670, it seems to have had but little attention, except from the Blackfeet Indians, until the early 1800s. Marias Pass, over the Divide on what is now the southern boundary, was not crossed by white men until 1810. The park terrain was slowly explored over the years, and in 1889 John Stevens surveyed Marias Pass for a rail line. Then, two years later, Great Northern Railroad built through this mile-high slit in the hills on its way to the Pacific Coast.

With a railroad circling its southern limits, the area came to be better known. But it was not until after the turn into the present century that a demand began to be made to conserve and protect this highly scenic region. In fact it was only in the spring of 1910 that its million acres were established as Glacier National Park.

Because of its exceptionally rugged nature, travel within its bounds was limited largely to hiking and horseback trips over its excellent trails. Then, in 1933, the famous Going-to-the-Sun Highway was completed from one side of the park to the other, a distance of 53 turning, twisting miles. It begins at St. Mary Entrance Station on U.S. 89 at the edge of the Blackfeet Indian Reservation. For several placid miles it hugs the north shore of gorgeous upper St. Mary Lake. Then after it passes Going-to-the-Sun Mountain at the lake's west end, it vaults upward by a series of switchbacks through 6600-foot Logan Pass, and on into the McDonald Creek region on the west side of the Continental Divide. Following down along that creek for 10 exciting miles, it then skirts the south shore of beautiful Lake McDonald, terminating just beyond its far end at the West Entrance Station.

By this means thousands have been able to see the very heart of this extraordinary park, who might otherwise have found it beyond their strength and endurance. Yet there are those who find the energy to push back away from the pavement and make use of the many well-equipped campgrounds throughout the park. These facilities have fireplaces and tables, and those adjoining the highways provide space for trailers. It is permissible to camp at sites other than regular campgrounds. But all who do so must obtain special fire permits. Liquid fuel stoves are preferable for separate camps, since forest fires are a decided menace in this park. Evidence of their destructiveness in the past may still be seen at many points. Overnight hiking trips without need of camping equipment can be arranged to such centers as Sperry or Granite Park Chalets, or Gunsight Lake Shelter. Some secluded points, however, cannot be seen except by pack trips into the back country, and horses, pack animals, and guides for such jaunts can be had at several locations.

The forest cover is for the most part evergreens, including several species each of cedar, hemlock, fir, spruce, and pine. The trees that shed their leaves include cottonwoods, larches, aspens, birches, and alders. There are enough of these latter so that the woods are highly colorful in early October.

The wildflowers, too, provide quite a display. Bear grass, which tops out in a burst of tiny white lilies, is probably the showiest of them all, and blooms through the warmer months. It starts first on the lowest valley floors and then mounts from one level to another as the season advances and the snowbanks disappear. The glacier lilies are also very showy and at their height in the early summer. The high alpine meadows are in full bloom by mid-July, and there are blossoms until the fall snows begin to arrive, for more than 1000 species of wildflowers can be found in the park.

There are sizable herds of mountain goats, moose, wapiti (elk), mule and whitetail deer, and both black and grizzly bears. A few bighorn mountain sheep can occasionally be seen, although the herds have fallen off in number in recent years. There are many beaver dams, and other fur bearers include the mink, marten, otter, and badger. There are, of course, mountain lions, but they are seldom seen, as is true with fishers and wolverines.

Both lakes and streams provide fish native to the cold mountain streams. Cutthroat, brook, rainbow, and Dolly Varden trout are extensively caught in flowing waters, while the large mackinaw trout are found in some of the lakes. There is launch service available during the summer on Josephine, McDonald, Swift-current, and Two Medicine lakes, and there are also rowboats for rent at different points on these four bodies of water.

The park season is from June 15 to September 10, although some facilities at high points are not available until July 1. There are numerous hotels, chalets, housekeeping and overnight cabins, and stores and eating places scattered through the park and along highways leading into it.

Principal means of access from Spokane, 290 miles away, and points in British Columbia, is the West Entrance via U.S. 2 and 93. Park headquarters are just inside, as is the western terminus of Going-to-the-Sun Highway. At the southeast is Two Medicine Entrance, convenient to U.S. 2 and 89, and 394 miles from Yellowstone National Park. On the east, along U.S. 89, is St. Mary Entrance, the eastern terminus of Going-to-the-Sun Highway. About 9 miles further north is a turnoff at Babb, leading in to Swiftcurrent Valley and the Many Glacier section. While U.S. 89 continues on into Alberta, there is another turnoff on to State Route 17 which goes to Chief Mountain, the entrance to Waterton Lakes National Park just over the international boundary.

Because of its close association with Glacier, many journey on into Canada to visit that section of the International Peace Park. The season there extends from May 1 to September 30, and the accommodations are varied and very good. The scenery is much like that in Glacier, and its mountains are equally rugged and similarly colorful. The reddish shales predominate and darken into wine and purple, while, for pleasing contrast, there are also outcroppings of various shades of green, and also some brilliant yellows. This Canadian section takes its name from Upper Waterton Lake, which lies most picturesquely in a deep trench between two towering mountain ranges.

ROCKY MOUNTAIN

THE great granite backbone of the continent is the Rocky Mountain System, which extends from the high plateau in New Mexico far away to the north into eastern Alaska. This huge chain of highlands, more than 2500 miles long, finds its greatest mass and magnificence in Colorado. There the land is stacked so high that about eight out of each ten peaks in the United States reaching to 14,000 feet are within the bounds of the Centennial State. There are no less than 52 of that height within its borders, and fully a thousand more points in the state reach to 10,000 feet or more.

Once the Rocky Mountains were nearly 2 miles higher. But they have been cut away by water and ice. The present Front Range, along which the Continental Divide winds its way, stands like a grim, jagged rampart, facing the plains that stretch east from Colorado to the Mississippi and beyond. Although some higher mountains lie to the west, they are no more noble and thrilling than those massed to the west and north of 14,255-foot Longs Peak, a king among mountains, dominating an area of supreme magnificence. A trip to its summit is truly a breath-taking experience.

The daring mountain men in search of beaver pelts came to know this thrilling "top o' the world" early in the 1800s. Jim Bridger, Uncle Dick Wootton, Kit Carson, and others of their kind followed rushing streams into the most secluded mountain valleys. But the footfalls in these uplands were principally those of Indians prowling in search of game until the Colorado gold rush of 1859. Then settlers began to find homes in Colorado, and in 1876 it became a state.

As early as 1860 Joel Estes had built a cabin in the eastern foothills of this mountain fastness. By 1865 tourists were pressing into this same area northwest of Denver, which soon became internationally famous for its big game. In 1871 the Earl of Dunraven came to hunt, but stayed on to buy land, and arranged to build the first hotel. His enthusiasm was very great, and he began to advocate a large preserve by which the beauty of this region might be retained. But it was not until 1915 that Congress acted and set aside what now totals a quarter million acres as Rocky Mountain National Park.

This block, which is roughly 25 miles from north to south and 18 from east to west, is surrounded by a protective ring of national forests. Its gentler slopes are to the west, where for some miles they spread down through the Big Meadows into one of the branches of the Colorado River. This is a lovely land, cresting on the far west in the chain of summits that make up the Never Summer Mountains. It is heavily wooded, and filled with many hurrying, glistening streams, emptying into rock-bound tarns and lakes. The entrance to this section is at Grand Lake, where there is a large village with hotels, cabins, stores, a post office, and saddle-horse corrals. This is reached from U.S. 40 at Granby, which is 80 miles from Denver.

From Grand Lake the motor road runs north along the Colorado River to Timber Creek. At Red Mountain it begins a series of switchbacks which carry it up through Milner Pass at 10,759 feet, and on to 11,797-foot Fall River Pass. Here, as the Trail Ridge Road, it becomes the highest continuous automobile highway in the United States. More than 4 miles of it rises above 12,000 feet in elevation, and a full 11 miles top the 11,000 foot timber line. From it, ranges of mountains stretch off as far as the eye can see, and forested canyons drop away to right and left.

Paralleling it for several miles between Fall River Pass and Horseshoe Park is one of the most sensational roads to be found in all the land. Known as the Fall River Road, it is a one-way trail up Fall River canyon, open to *upbound* travel only. It is recommended only to the experienced mountain driver in search of the thrills of motoring in an earlier era. Some delight in driving west over this demanding cut off, and then circling back to the east over the very scenic Trail Ridge Road.

This latter, which actually takes transcontinental route U.S. 34 through the park, splits at Deer Ridge Junction, its northern spur going on to Estes Park Village, the chief eastern entrance. A southern spur drops down through Beaver Meadows to the Thompson River Entrance. Here one fork runs along lovely Thompson River to connect with Estes Park. The other fork climbs back to the west to glacier-formed, blue-green Bear Lake, almost encircled by a series of high peaks. From here, a network of trails fans out into the surrounding high country.

While considerable numbers see the park only from the motor roads, many take to the trails which provide the real opportunities to explore and know its countless wonders. While the majority of them are intended for travel on horseback, there are sections where they are suitable for foot travel only, and then by those experienced in and equal to strenuous mountain work. Some should be attempted only by the most capable hikers. For longer trips guides are strongly recommended, and the advice of the chief ranger should be sought in making plans. Horses and trail gear can be rented at most of the villages and camps, where guides may also be engaged.

The accommodations both within and close by the park are very extensive, and include hotels, motels, lodges, cabins, and simple camps. There are several public campgrounds within park limits. Those at Glacier Basin, Aspenglen, Endovalley, and Timber Creek, embracing about 300 sites, provide water and sanitary facilities, but no electricity. There is provision at them for trailers. The grounds at Longs Peak and Wild Basin are smaller, and have only minimum facilities. There is also a larger recreational area at Shadow Mountain Lake and Granby Reservoir, near the Grand Lake Entrance, with campgrounds at Big Rock and Monarch Lake.

The park is a wildlife sanctuary, and its larger

tenants include elk, deer, black bears, coyotes, bobcats, mountain lions, and the Rocky Mountain bighorn sheep. Herds of the latter are not infrequently seen at Sheep Lake, Milner Pass, and on Specimen Mountain. Beaver dams are common, marmots hurry in and out of their burrows along roads and trails, and the large squirrel and chipmunk population are ever busy with their affairs. There are more than 200 varieties of birds, and some 700 of wildflowers. While the carpet of trees in the lowlands is mostly evergreens, there are enough poplars and quaking aspens to gild the woods in the fall. There are guided field trips, nature walks, and illustrated evening talks to help heighten the visitor's enjoyment.

While some park roads are kept open throughout the year, snow prevents cross-park travel between late October and early June. There are ski runs at Hidden Valley about 12 miles west of the entrance at Estes Park, together with a tow and a shelter cabin.

HAWAII

THE Hawaiian Islands rose from the sea at some time in the past in a series of volcanic eruptions. And the burstings forth that brought them into being must have been most violent ones, for these many bodies of land stand in water more than 3 miles deep, and the conelike mountains on some of them thrust up another 2½ miles above the level of the sea. The islands vary considerably in size, and the larger were not only outpourings of lava and ashes, but enlarged by coral growths.

The most easterly and largest in the group is Hawaii, covering more than 4000 square miles. On it are several volcanoes. The greatest of them, and supposedly the largest volcanic mass in the world today, is Mauna Loa (mou'-neh-low'-eh), or "long mountain." This vast dome, whose summit crater is called Mokuaweoweo (mah-koo-ah-we'-oh-we'-oh), rises in the center of the island to a height of 13,680 feet.

It is still active, but between its eruptions has rest periods that last anywhere from several months to 9 or 10 years. While it has never maintained a lava lake within its crater, it has poured out more lava during the last century than any other volcano in the world. Its flows occupy more than 2000 square miles, or over half the area of the island, and extend from its snow-capped summit to the ocean bottom more than 31,000 feet below down its huge flanks. While many of its eruptions are confined within its crater, others manage to blast huge cracks in the mountainside well down from the summit, and spew forth fiery, molten rock.

Such a breach occurred well up on the northeast ridge back in 1881, and the lava that gushed forth flowed down to the edge of the city of Hilo, more than 30 miles distant. Again in 1942, following a series of heavy earthquakes, burning, flaming lava squirted from a great crack in the mountain's shoulder in a series of fountains, and ran to within 12 miles of Hilo. In 1950 a mighty fissure 13 miles long opened up, and during 23 days more than a billion tons of lava issued from it. In some places it sped toward the sea in scorching rivers flowing six miles an hour, while one rivulet, years ago, is said to have traveled at a rate of 40 miles an hour.

Associated with Mauna Loa, and lying about 23 miles to the east of its much higher neighbor, is the dome of Kilauea (kee'-loo-ay'-ah). Its summit has collapsed, and the now shallow trough which forms its upper reaches is spoken of as a *caldera*. Within it is one of the most fearful of the many wonders in all our national parks. It is the vast Halemaumau (hah-lay-mou'-mou) pit, or "the house of everlasting fire." This is a lake of gurgling, boiling lava 1750° hot on its surface, which sometimes wells up and overflows onto the crater floor. At other times it is sucked back within the earth, and sinks almost out of sight. Then the walls crumble and avalanche into the depths of the yawning cavern, sometimes letting great quantities of water cascade into the depths. When this happens there are violent steam explosions which hurl out tons of rock and dust. Such a blast heaped death and destruction upon a native army in 1790. Bare footprints in wet volcanic ash hurled six miles away from the pit still give testimony to this time in the long ago when disaster suddenly struck.

An enormous steam eruption in 1924 gouged out a much larger pit some 3000 feet in diameter, and 1300 feet deep. Within eight years a series of eruptions had raised the pit floor more than 500 feet. But in 1952 there was great activity, and in a little over 4 months the bottom of the pit had been raised another 300 feet. Two years later, at the end of May 1954, a fall-in of the pit walls set off a violent eruption. Soon a fountain was hurling lava some 650 feet into the air, and not long afterward a half-mile row of fountains began spraying molten material 100 feet or more above their surroundings. But this time the built up pressures were soon released, and this brilliant display quieted down after 4 days. In 1955 there were 6 terrifying weeks during which streaming fountains and spurting vents well down Kilauea's sides below the *caldera* rim destroyed gardens, orchards, and highways. Thus the two summits in that portion of Hawaii National Park lying on the island of Hawaii are intensely active, and likely to be heard from at any time.

About 30 miles northwest across Alenuihaha Channels lies the island of Maui (mou'-ih), second largest of the Hawaiian group. Crowning its eastern end is the 10,000-foot peak of Haleakala (hah-lay-ah-kah'-lah)—the "House of the Sun"—and fourth largest slumbering volcano in the world. Its immense crater, one of the largest known, forms the second section of the Hawaii National Park established in 1916. It is very old and, if not actually dead, is in its final stages of activity, for its last-known eruption was about 200 years ago. During a long period it has perhaps been very quiet, and erosion and an eating away by the elements have enlarged its crater. Yet as it was slowly dying down eruptions pushed up cinder cones in its floor, and flooded the area with lava flows. Now the great summit depression extends over some 19 square miles. Much of the floor lies 2500 or more feet below the rim that circles it, the walls of the latter being higher to the north and west. Clouds formed by the trade winds often drift in from the east, and fill the colossal *caldera*. Sometimes visitors standing along the western rim in the late afternoon will be thrilled to see their own shadows cast in gigantic relief on the sea of cloud before them, with these darkened silhouettes framed in a circular rainbow. This marvel is very much like the Brocken Specter which occurs at some points in the Alps.

But there are other things to see and enjoy within the two sections of the park besides volcanoes and the results of volcanic action. Plants native to each of these islands are not found anywhere else in the whole world. For instance, in the Haleakala Crater grows the strange, rare silversword. It throws up a "pincushion" of long, daggerlike leaves that look as though they were

Western Ways Photo

Above: Mount McKinley, here seen from the north, is the greatest single mountain mass on earth, rising higher above its own base than any other. The water is Wonder Lake. *Below left:* Forests of giant tree ferns cover large areas in and near Hawaii National Park. *Below right:* Mount Lassen in the spring, snow patches still clothing this slowly dying volcano.

Photo by Werner Stoy *National Park Service from Western Ways*

Above: Air view of Mother Nature's greatest excavation job, the Grand Canyon. For some 217 miles this huge trench varies from four to eighteen miles wide, and up to a mile deep. *Below left:* Viewing Grand Canyon from the South Rim as the sinking sun's shadows lengthen. *Below right:* A party on muleback picking its way down the side of Grand Canyon.

formed of silver. From its center a flower stalk thrusts up 6 or more feet, and on it opens up a vast bloom made up of countless purple flowers. Thoughtless visitors almost destroyed this regal plant, which under protection is slowly establishing itself again.

In the rain forests on the lower slopes grow the koa, a light-tinted mahogany tree, the ohia with its gorgeous pompoms of terra-cotta-colored flowers, and the monkeypod with its pink blooms. The roads and trails lead through tree ferns up to 40 feet tall, and are bordered with displays of fuchsias, ginger, nasturtiums, and hibiscus, a tropical wonderland.

Flitting through this tropical growth are many birds of brilliant plumage, and bearing such interesting native names as: amakihi, apapane, elepaio, iiwi, io, and pueo. Japanese green and American ring-necked pheasants are common, as are quail, Kentucky cardinals, English skylarks, and other imported birds. Most animals now living wild were also imported—pigs from Hawaii, goats from England, and mongooses from India.

The Haleakala section of the park is about 110 air miles from Honolulu, while the remainder at Kilauea-Mauna Loa is some 200 miles away. The former is reached by paved road from Kahului, and the latter by a highway from Hilo. There are several passenger plane flights daily between Honolulu and these other two cities.

This park, divided between two of the islands, may seem very remote to many, and perhaps a little hard to reach from the more widely known sections of the Hawaiian group. But all who have been to sample the wonders which it contains will agree that they are sufficiently unique to make the effort abundantly worth while.

LASSEN VOLCANIC

Our volcanic national parks include Lassen, Crater Lake, Mount Rainier, Yellowstone, and Hawaii. The first three of them are spaced along the Cascade Mountains, which run from northeastern California through Oregon, and on to the northern edge of Washington. This whole range was volcanic, and resulted from a great outpouring of lava which formed a plateau about 8000 feet high. Then upon it peaks were formed by further eruptions which heaped up cones of lava and ash forced through vent holes. Some of these volcanoes were big, while others were little. Many of the latter disappeared under the growing bulk of their mightier neighbors, and some of the most celebrated among those that remain today are mounts Baker, Rainier, Adams, St. Helens, Hood, Shasta, Lassen, and the almost vanished Mount Mazama. Lassen Peak, standing at the long ridge's southern end, is perhaps the only one among them still active enough to have further eruptions.

It took its name from the stouthearted Peter Lassen, Danish settler who had a ranch near its base even before the area became a part of the United States. Its 10,453 feet stood well above its surroundings, and provided an effective landmark by which Lassen piloted westbound parties from Humboldt Sink over the high ridges into Sacramento Valley. Yet it probably had no plume of smoke or steam at its summit a hundred years ago, for previous to the activity which began in 1914 it seems to have been asleep most of the time during several hundred years.

But on May 30, 1914, the mountain awoke with a shudder of earth-shaking explosions. Although activity continued during the next seven years, none was too destructive and the flow of lava was not large, especially when contrasted with the fountains that have several times in recent years poured huge lakes of molten rock from Mauna Loa on the island of Hawaii.

About a year after this activity began, glowing lava did squeeze up and fill the bottom of the crater and then leak out through a low place in the west rim wall, flowing 1000 feet or more down the mountain's side. The resulting heat melted the late-lying snows, and the floods coursing down the northeast slope caused great mud flows. They also loosened huge boulders that bounced down Lassen's broad flanks and rolled 5 and 6 miles out into Hat Creek and Lost Creek valleys. A few days later there were more mud flows, followed by a hot blast that poured down the northeast slope with such violence that it flattened trees 3 miles below the crater. A column of vapor and ash rose some 5 miles into the air, and the devastation in the area was so great that after more than 40 years the forest cover is but slowly beginning to heal the wounds.

By the end of 1915, the reawakened giant had about spent its force, and some scientists believe this fairly brief activity may have been a sort of dying gasp. But all this volcanic action had taken place within the United States proper. So the lessening activities that kept up until 1921 received quite a little attention, and were sufficient to keep this mountain in the list of *active* volcanoes in the opinion of many. Lassen Peak and Cinder Cone had been set apart as national monuments in 1907, and Lassen Volcanic National Park was established in 1916. It now embraces about 163 square miles in northeastern California, 100 miles below the Oregon line, and 130 north of Sacramento.

Three miles to the southwest of Lassen Peak there formerly stood an even greater cone, 12 miles in diameter. It once rose fully 4000 feet above what remains of it today in the steam and sulphur vents and hot springs at Sulphur Works. Its upper portion seems to have collapsed and withdrawn into the earth, leaving a great bowl, or *caldera*. Much of its rim has been eroded away, but portions still remain to form Brokeoff Mountain, Mount Diller, Mount Conrad, and the base of Pilot Mountain.

Toward the northeast corner of the park is 6913-foot Cinder Cone. Because of its very great regularity of outline, it is thought to have been built up after the glaciers had melted away. It was active for a brief period in 1850-51, but had erupted vigorously at a much earlier time, when it deposited some rather fantastic lava beds to the east and south. Also at the base of this cone on its southern side is a series of colorful "painted" dunes.

Two and three miles north of Lassen Peak are the unusual Chaos Crags. These are lofty plugs of stiffened lava forced up by great pressure through volcanic necks, or openings, until they stood like 1800-foot cliffs. Water seeping into the necks set off violent steam explosions, which undermined and shattered these huge stone stacks. The great loosened fragments slid down and spread out over 2½ square miles in a vast rock pile called Chaos Jumbles. Other interesting points to visit are the *thermal* areas, with their hot springs and steam vents, at Bumpass Hell, Little Hot Springs Valley, Devil's Kitchen, and Boiling Springs Lake.

Much of the park is carpeted with a heavy evergreen forest, although there are large areas, too, of chaparral thickets, principally manzanita, tobacco brush, and chinquapin. There are enough aspens, cottonwoods, willows, and alders along the creek beds so that there is a warmth of color in the fall; and there are several hundred varieties of wildflowers, which bloom between May and late September. The crimson snow plant livens the meadows in the spring, and it and other flowers follow the melting snow up into the high country. The Indian paintbrush, scarlet bugler, bleeding heart, mimulus, and tiger lily are very common, and the subalpine uplands are aglow in mid-August with lupine, pentstemon, laurel, and heather.

Among the larger animals the mule and black-tailed deer are most commonly seen. There are black bears but they generally keep out of sight. There are many species of birds ranging all the way up to bald eagles;

101

and trout fishing is good in the streams, while there are catfish in Manzanita and Reflection lakes. Lassen, like all the other national parks, is of course a sanctuary for the creatures living within its boundaries. Under such protection, the different species tend to increase both in number and in friendliness. Many may be approached by visitors and fed, and, in a few cases, even petted. So it is hard for some to understand the warning of the park authorities to keep entirely clear of the animals in these preserves. In this connection, the ground squirrels and chipmunks in Lassen provide an example of the good intentions behind the warnings. These tiny, busy, appealing little rodents set up a strong urge in some to feed and play with them. But even in their case it is recommended that there be no actual contact, for some of them carry highly dangerous diseases, which can be transmitted to humans.

Much of the western portion of the park can be reached from Lassen Peak Highway. There are unpaved roads running well into the eastern half, which is also served by an extensive network of trails. Seven campgrounds have been provided, three of which are reached from the main highway, and the others over service roads or trails.

A lodge, bungalows, housekeeping cabins, and

floored tents are available during the summer season, or from late May through September. The park highway is customarily usable over its entire length from June to late October, and is kept open for a reasonable distance inside both the Manzanita and Sulphur Works Entrances at all times.

The park offers excellent skiing, particularly for cross-country trips. There is a tow at the run in the Sulphur Works Ski Area, and equipment can be rented there. There is also a warming house and refreshment stand. The season begins in December, and in some years there are still usable patches of snow at high points as late as August.

MOUNT McKINLEY

THE highest point on the North American Continent is a huge mountain peak about 250 miles below the Arctic Circle in south-central Alaska. The Indians called it *Denali*, "home of the sun," and they claimed it was the enormous rock hurled by one of their gods at his wife who was attempting to run away.

It was 1902 before white men first set foot upon its ponderous slopes, and 1910 before they had made their way to the summit of this 20,269-foot giant, named McKinley for our twenty-fifth president, who was assassinated in 1901. As they came to know this majestic mountain better, they at last realized that it was actually the loftiest peak above its base in the world. It towers some 17,000 feet above the broad plateau on its north and west sides. To the south and west of it along the upper reaches of the Alaska Range stand 14,580-foot Mount Hunter, 17,317-foot Mount Foraker, and 11,670-foot Mount Russell. To the east are Brooks Mountain and Mount Mather, both well above 11,000 feet.

This gigantic block of mountains supports a tremendous glacial system that clutches it like an immense octopus, and makes McKinley difficult to reach except from the west. The timberline reaches but a short distance up its flanks, for two thirds of the way down from its summit it is deep in snow and ice throughout the year. The largest northward-flowing glaciers of the Alaska Range have their beginning on the cold, ice-encrusted slopes of Mount McKinley and Mount Foraker. Yet those that creep down so very slowly from the southern slope are far greater, since they are fed from the very moist winds that blow up from the Pacific Ocean.

Here stood a great natural scenic wonder, which deserved to be kept safe and unspoiled for the enjoyment of future generations. So, in 1917, it was established as the thirteenth of our national parks by an act of Congress. Five years later it was expanded to cover an area of 2645 square miles, while further extensions to the north and east in 1932 brought it up to 1,939,493 acres. It is thus the second largest of our parks, exceeded only by Yellowstone.

Since it tops all other summits on the continent, and is the tallest mountain above its base in all the world, it has always tempted the adventurous to climb it. Yet it has been scaled only on five occasions over the years, according to official records. Its last two conquests are somewhat unique. In 1942, in the early part of the war, seven members of the Army Test Expedition who were living high on the mountain, trying out winter equipment and supplies, ascended both the north and south peaks. Then, in 1947, Mrs. Bradford Washburn and her husband, together with seven other men, reached the top. She was the first woman ever to do so. Many others would no doubt like to make the attempt, but only those with superior climbing ability and extensive knowledge of what may be encountered on the demanding trip can hope to gain the necessary permission. Attempts in the past which seemed certain of success have had to be given up when quick changes in the weather have brought long-lasting blizzards or killing sub-zero temperatures.

But the park has other features besides its snow-clad mountain peaks and glaciers to attract visitors. It is a highly important game refuge, and the home of great numbers of caribou. These large, flat-horned deer are sometimes seen singly, or in pairs, or again in herds of several hundred anywhere from the low-lying barrens far up on the high slopes of the ridges. Their European cousins, the "Santa Claus" reindeer, have been placed in the park, and this darker, shorter-legged creature, almost top-heavy with antlers, is increasing in numbers rapidly. Caribou trails are common, and often lead to salt licks or to stands of willows, the bark of which is used by these beasts to rub the velvet from their antlers.

Far larger is the big Alaska moose, whose immense fore quarters may rise 7½ feet above the ground, while his broad, fan-shaped antlers may have a 5-foot spread. The larger males weigh up to 1700 pounds, and so are four or five times as heavy as a caribou or reindeer. The park, too, is the home of the big, rugged Toklat grizzly bear, who pockmarks the tundra digging out ground squirrels. One may also see red foxes, wolverines, timber wolves, and an occasional lynx. But the most handsome beast is easily the Dall sheep, slightly smaller than the Rocky Mountain bighorn. But it is very white of body, with slender, widely curved tan-colored horns. The older rams stand about 40 inches high at the shoulders, and weigh up to 200 pounds. The lambing time is May, and by early summer small bands of lambs may be seen gamboling in the mountain meadows under the watchful eyes of the mother ewes. They soon learn to be very sure-footed, and even small, growing legs are able to make jumps up to 6 or more feet in height. In the warmer months, the herds spend much time along Igloo Creek and the East Fork and Toklat rivers, which are crossed by the Denali Highway through the park.

There are well over 100 types of birds, most of which nest within park limits. One of the hardest to see among them is the surfbird, which, as the weather grows colder, flies off to spend its winters at the southern tip of South America, 10,000 miles away. There are grouse, the ptarmigan with feathered toes that serve as snowshoes, and the deadly, day-flying hawk owl. Other powerful hunters are the shaggy-legged gyrfalcon and the fearless, tiny pigeon hawk. There are also ducks, and many bright plumaged song birds.

Fishing is good in McKinley National Park. The true game fish of the streams is the Arctic grayling, while the Mackinaw trout in Wonder Lake often run to 24 inches or longer.

The commonest tree is the white spruce, and there are cottonwoods, aspens, and willows along the streams in the lower valleys. About a dozen varieties of low-growing shrubs make up the thickets that carpet extensive areas. There are quite a number of flowering plants, some of which cover extensive patches in the meadowlands.

The park can be reached only by air or railroad, and there is a landing field with a 3000-foot runway near the park station on the Alaska Railroad, which runs from Seward and Anchorage on tidewater to Fairbanks. There is also a hotel close by, and headquarters are at Mile 2 on the Trans-Park Highway. This gravel auto road is now 95 miles long, extending 6 miles beyond the north boundary to Kantishna and swinging south along the railroad 45 miles to Summit, just outside the eastern limits. Many visitors ship in private cars over the railroad for use in the park. The trail system is not extensive; but there are a number of cabins in river bottoms along the north boundary that are easily reached and much used.

Winter snows are relatively light, although temperatures sometimes drop to 45° and 50° below zero. In the summer, the principal season for visitors, there are 18 or more hours of sunshine, and the thermometer ranges from 60° to 80°.

This is the second of the three parks which lie outside the continental limits of the United States and so will seem to many to be at a very great distance. It is most unfortunate that this sublime mountain and its surroundings cannot be more easily reached by far greater numbers, for the area is surely worthy of a visit. But vacations seem to grow long and reach further afield with the years, and there is little doubt but that the time will soon come when far greater numbers will journey to Alaska and include a trip to Mount McKinley National Park as though it were a "must."

ACADIA

IN 1604, three years before there was a settlement at Jamestown, Samuel de Champlain sailed up our eastern seacoast. He visited a number of points, among them a large, rocky island, the largest along what is now the Maine Coast. He named it *Isle des Mont Déserts,* or the "island of lonely mountains." Now called Mount Desert Island, it was well within the confines of *Acadia,* the province which the French King claimed began in the latitude of the city of Philadelphia and extended north to the Gulf of St. Lawrence.

A French mission settlement was planted on the island of lonely mountains a few years later. But it was destroyed in 1613 by an armed vessel from Jamestown, commanded by Captain Samuel Argall, who that same year kidnaped the Indian princess Pocahontas. This contest at Mount Desert Island was the first in a struggle between the English and the French for control of North America that lasted for a century and a half.

In 1688, Louis XIV of France gave the island as a feudal fief to the Sieur de la Mothe Cadillac, who later founded Detroit and served as Governor of Louisiana. While that portion of French Acadia finally came under the control of the Province of Massachusetts, the eastern portion of Mount Desert Island was finally given to the granddaughter of Cadillac following the Revolution, as a token of gratitude for French aid during that war. Both this large grant and another to the western half of the island were sold piece by piece to settlers. Then, during the early 1800s, fishing hamlets and lumber camps began to bring people to this remote area.

Following the Civil War, Mount Desert Island slowly became a summer resort. It was a trifle primitive at first, but finally Bar Harbor came to rival Newport, down the coast in Rhode Island, as a social center. Many wealthy and influential people had summer homes there. They realized the scenic beauty and historical background of this region that had formerly been difficult to reach. With improved transportation, they knew it might soon be overrun by great numbers of people. So in 1901 a group of residents set up an organization to acquire and hold in trust for public enjoyment large tracts of unused land. By 1914 they had assembled about 6000 acres. This was offered to the government for a federal park, and in 1916 President Wilson proclaimed it the Sieur de Monts National Monument. Early in 1919 it was established as Lafayette National Park, the first park east of the Mississippi River, and also the first in which the land had been donated to the government rather than having been taken from the public domain. Its name was changed to Acadia in 1929, to preserve the original designation given the region as early as 1604.

This fine plant and animal sanctuary now totals close to 30,000 acres. Originally it was principally upland areas on the two halves of Mount Desert Island, which is cut nearly in two by Somes Sound, the only true fiord along our Atlantic Coast. There were also some ocean-front sections; and both blocks have been slowly added to. Then a considerable section of Schoodic Point, a headland to the east across Frenchman Bay, was added. More recently, about one half of the Isle au Haut, which lies in the ocean about 20 miles southwest of Mount Desert, has been taken in.

The park thus embraces both land and sea, and also mountains, lakes, woodlands, rocky promontories, and sandy beaches—a wide variety of natural features. Here also the trees, flowers, and plant life of the Northern and Temperate Zones grow side by side. Wildflowers are of many types and are in bloom from early spring well into the fall. The trees and forest growth include many species, some of which are found as far south as the highlands of Georgia, while others are common to Newfoundland and Labrador. Some of the bogs and headlands support plants generally found in the Hudson Bay and subarctic regions.

Highest point on Mount Desert Island is the summit of Cadillac Mountain, which reaches an elevation of 1530 feet. A motor road from the park entrance at Hulls Cove circles through the eastern section, passes along the ocean front, and then climbs to the lookout atop the mountain. From it there are beautiful views seaward and also over the park preserve. Bubble Pond, Jordan Pond, and Eagle Lake all lie along this main park road.

The portion of the park in the western half of the island is reached by state highways into that area, and then by secondary roads into the different sections. Seawall Campground, on the ocean front near Bass Harbor Head Lighthouse, may be reached over State Route 102. Black Woods Campground, also within sight of the ocean, is convenient to State Route 3, and not far from the Seal Harbor Entrance. These are well equipped, and open for use from June 1 to October 1, although the park may be entered throughout the year. There are picnic grounds at several points on Mount Desert Island, and one on Schoodic Point.

This latter section is reached by State Route 186, which circles Schoodic Peninsula, and connects with U.S. 1 at several points. Mount Desert Island itself is tied to the mainland by a causeway and bridges over which State Route 3 from Ellsworth passes, and there is also connection with U.S. 1. There is an airport at Trenton near the end of the causeway, and railroad and bus line connections can be made at Ellsworth.

While there are no accommodations other than picnic and campgrounds within the park itself, there are excellent facilities of all kinds in the villages on Mount Desert Island, and in neighboring communities on the mainland. Although the motor road system affords access to much of the original section of the park, there are also about 50 miles of bridle paths, and 100 miles of trails. Some of these latter can prove rather strenuous for hikers. A number of planned activities have been arranged to make visitors better acquainted with the park's offerings. These include auto caravan tours guided by a Ranger-naturalist, nature walks, sea cruises, and trips to Islesford Historical Museum on Little Cranberry Island.

The new ferry service which transports automobiles and their passengers between Bar Harbor and Yarmouth, Nova Scotia, will bring many more vacationers onto Mount Desert Island. A goodly number of them, it is to be hoped, will include time enough in their schedule so a visit may be made to this, the most easterly of the parks on the United States mainland.

GRAND CANYON

In 1540 a large party of Spaniards, greedy for easy wealth, pressed up out of Mexico intent upon locating and seizing the seven mythical cities of Cibola, supposedly built of pure gold. While this was to prove a most disappointing and even tragic venture, yet one of its scouting parties was to have a peculiar thrill. Its members became the first white men to gaze upon "by far the most sublime of all earthly spectacles"—the Grand Canyon of the Colorado River, located in what is today the northwest corner of Arizona.

What they saw spread out before and below them was the world's mightiest gorge, cut in solid rock over countless ages by one of America's most determined, hardest-working rivers. This is no simple, even if deep-cut, trench, but a thousand square miles of pyramids, minarets, and strange objects carved from the most colorful rocks. It is 217 miles long, from 4 to 18 miles wide, often a mile deep, and spreads before the viewer about one billion years of the earth's long history. Here the forces of nature have been turned loose to cut through layer after layer of the earth's surface that had once been laid down during millions upon millions of years on the bottom of some great arm of the ocean. Then these strata had slowly been raised high above the level of the sea, and rain, snow, frost, and ice, plus running water, had gone to work to wear them down. A great stream gathered the rainfall dropped from the clouds upon several thousand square miles, and began to cut a furrow, and then a trench, and at last this immense canyon. When the Spaniards looked down upon it, thousands of feet below them, they called the stream the *Colorado,* which means "red," for it was red with its great burden of soil and finely ground rock. Even in our own time this tireless river bears a half million tons—12,000 freight cars full—of silt through the canyon on an average day. When it is in flood with melting snow water in early summer, it may drive 60 times its normal load on toward Lake Mead, formed by the Hoover Dam some 260 miles downstream.

Although there is still a reservation in the depths of the canyon, where the remnant of the Havasupai Indians dwell, extensive use of the area by the native people came several centuries ago when great numbers in the Southwest began to live in large communal dwellings, often built in the caverns in canyon walls. More than 600 sites at which such pueblos had been constructed in ages past have been found. It was an untamed, little frequented region as the West was explored and began to fill with settlers. This enormous hole in the ground, along with the wild, surging river deep within it, formed an extensive barrier. A few trappers and prospectors ventured down its dizzy walls, and cattlemen finally made some use of the tableland along its rims. Stories of its unbelievable wonders were probably doubted by many of their early hearers. Then, in 1869, the courageous geologist, John Wesley Powell, led a party on a voyage of great danger and hardship down the Colorado River through the Grand Canyon. His reliable report brought more and more hardy souls to the rims of this profound abyss.

Its popularity began to grow as the railroad at last made it more easy to visit. Those who gazed out over this fantastic spectacle returned to sing its praises, and some to demand that the federal government take it in charge. But many obstacles stood in the way, and it was only after 33 years of determined effort that it became our fifteenth park in 1919, after having been a national monument for 11 years. Just a little over 1000 square miles of the most showy part of the canyon were placed on a park basis. Then, in 1932, an additional 196,000 acres of queer, grotesque wilderness immediately west of the park were established as a new Grand Canyon National Monument. This, in turn, adjoins the nearly 3000 square miles of the Lake Mead National Recreation Area. To the east of Grand Canyon National Park lies the picturesque Painted Desert and Hopi and Navajo reservations. This whole remarkable region is deserving of its many visitors.

The eastern half of the park is far more accessible. So, too, is the South Rim, which is but 59 miles from Williams and 110 from Flagstaff on heavily travelled U.S. 66. Also, it is but 6900 feet in elevation, and so 1250 feet lower than the North Rim, which makes considerable difference in weather conditions during the colder months. The South Rim is open all the year, but many North Rim lodges are open only from June 18 to September 10, while more limited facilities are available from mid-May only to mid-October.

On the South Rim it is possible for the highway to closely follow the edge of the canyon for some 28 miles, which permits a number of lookout points from which there are breath-taking views. Most of these are fairly close to the river, some 4500 feet below. The western portion of the South Rim may be reached at three points by a dirt road. At its end, at Hilltop, there is a trail down to the Havasupai Indian Reservation.

The North Rim is reached over State Route 67, which turns off from U.S. 89 about 45 miles north of the park village on Bright Angel Point. This pavement swings around to Point Imperial in the northeast portion of the park. It then follows through a dense forest, but reasonably close to the canyon edge, down the Walhalla Plateau to Cape Royal, from which one of the finest views of all may be had. While Bright Angel Point on the North Rim and Grand Canyon Village on the South Rim are but 10 miles apart as the crow flies, it requires more than 200 miles of driving to get from one point to the other by car.

For those more than 12 years old, and weighing less than 190 pounds, there is a shorter and far more exciting way of making this journey. It is by mule back over the transcanyon Kaibab Trail, and takes two days from rim to rim, with a stopover for the night at Phantom Ranch beyond the Kaibab Suspension Bridge over the Colorado River at the bottom of the gorge. The bridge is 440 feet long but only one mule wide. Yet it is the only one in more than 300 miles along this unruly stream. A less rigorous trip is down the Bright Angel Trail, which drops some 4400 feet from the South Rim to the river in but 8 miles by means of a series of switchbacks. A return can be made the same afternoon, or a night may be spent in the depth of the canyon and the ascent completed the next day up the equally rugged Kaibab Trail. This is the only way in which the most spectacular of our parks can be seen from both top and bottom.

Beside muleback trips into its depths, arrangements can also be made for airplane flights over this whole fantastic region. But the Park Service does much to heighten the visitor's enjoyment. Typical is the free-admission observation station at Yavapai Point, where there are specimens, diagrams, relief models, and telescopes focused on outstanding features, together with a naturalist to explain it all. The Wayside Museum tells the story of man in the Southwest, and the many campfire programs are excellent. The Hopi Indians stage a ceremonial dance each afternoon at the Hopi House. It really takes several days for the mind and even the eyes to absorb the wonders along either rim.

Hotels, lodges, motor courts, and other accommodations are maintained on both the North and South Rims. Those in the latter area are more extensive, and are open all the year. There are two public campgrounds on each of the rims.

Zion National Park, just over the line into Utah, is but a 125-mile drive from the North Rim and 250 miles from the South Rim. Bryce Canyon National Park, also in Utah, is about 45 miles farther.

ZION

Although the Spaniards and the fur trappers had made hurried journeys through southwestern Utah, that region had little real attention until the arrival of the Mormons. In 1858 they began to settle in the area, which they called "Dixie," and that same year one of their scouts found his way into a very remarkable canyon. Its almost vertical walls, nearly a mile high at some places, and vivid with color, are the work of the north fork of the Virgin River. This eager, determined river had cut this deep gash in the huge Kolob Plateau, and is still hard at work. Each day it hurries along some 200 freight carloads of sediment, dumping its cargo of red mud into Lake Mead, formed by the Colorado at Hoover Dam. John Wesley Powell, conqueror of the Grand Canyon, visited this marvel in 1872 and gave the north fork of the river the difficult name of "Mukuntuweap," by which the canyon was called when it was proclaimed a national monument in 1909. But Brigham Young, who had seen its glories years earlier, had named it "Zion," and when it became a park in 1919 it was so designated.

Many people drive into and through this canyon in closed cars and miss most of its majestic beauty. It is often no more than a half mile wide at the bottom, and perhaps a mile from crest to crest. Unless the car is frequently stopped, and those in it step out, walk about, and let their gaze run up and down the sides of this mighty trench, much remains unseen. The tremendous stone monuments lining the gorge, with such interesting names as Great White Throne, Angels Landing, Temple of Sinawava, Mountain of the Sun, Great Organ, the Three Patriarchs—deserve careful study. It is said that every known color can be found at some point upon them.

At their base the grays and yellows of the Belted Shales blend nicely with the green of the cottonwoods, piñons, and cedars that carpet the canyon floor, and struggle up its lower slopes. Above is a band that is mostly brown and gray, and which supports the stratum of red mixed with lavender and purple which also tints the Painted Desert lying to the south. Higher up are the deep-dyed Vermilion Cliffs, which crop out at various points over quite an area and provide great streaks of brilliant red. At places this giddy scarlet sash may be 2000 feet broad, and is usually capped by a deep layer of rocks of glistening white, frosted on some of the summits with touches of brown and crimson rock, trimmed with the scattered green of western pines.

At many places the various colors have run down the faces of the cliffs and left stains like Roman stripes. Erosion by rain and frost has sculptured numerous fanciful and startling designs which, with the riot of colors, make the park a veritable fairyland. This great scenic wealth is closely packed into about 6 miles of Zion Canyon, with other wondrous views along a similar length of Clear Creek Canyon, which enters it from the east. The park is thus relatively small, embracing but 147 square miles, yet well worth a visit.

Within its boundaries there are some 20 miles of pavement. One road leads from the South Entrance through to the foot of the Temple of Sinawava at the north end of Zion Canyon, a distance of 8 miles. At its lower end, near park headquarters, it is joined by the exciting Zion-Mount Carmel Highway, which runs 11½ miles to the East Entrance and on to the important north-south route U.S. 89. This road climbs

Above: View across Frenchman Bay from top of Cadillac Mountain in Acadia National Park. Group of houses in the foreground is Bar Harbor. Part of the park borders the bay.   *Below right:* One of Zion Park's most popular feature is the Great White Throne, rising to 6744 feet.   *Below left:* One of the Three Patriarchs grouped along the south wall of startling Zion Canyon.

Union Pacific Railroad Photo

Above: This example of fantastic erosion on the wall below Sunset Point is an excellent sample of nature's handiwork in Bryce Canyon. Colors here run chiefly to pink. *Below:* Hot Springs National Park lies in this well-forested, lake-dotted Ouachita Mountain area.

Spa News Bureau

by a series of switchbacks up into Clear Creek Valley. Then, after plunging through a mile-long tunnel, it continues to work its winding way up out of the canyon onto the top of the mesa and beyond the limits of the park. Views from it are truly breath-taking.

There are also about 26 miles of trails leading to interesting sections and special vantage points. A part of this trail system can be used throughout the year, although some sections are closed by snow during the colder months. A wide variety of trips is possible, both as to length and with regard to demands upon the user. Some are over fairly flat stretches where the going is easy, while others require greater effort. Some are highly strenuous, either on foot or horseback, and one or two should be attempted only by the most experienced mountain climbers. Saddle horses and guides are available during the summer.

Although limited in area, Zion's lower reaches are much like the desert region which spreads away to the south, while its upper portions resemble the spruce-covered highland country on to the north. This fosters quite a variety of wildlife. Mule deer are often found grazing at points on the floor of the canyon in the evening. Foxes and coyotes are sometimes seen along the trails, and occasionally a bobcat or even a mountain lion, although they tend to keep out of sight as far as possible. There are several species of birds; and many visitors unaccustomed to them find the lizards quite interesting. The blue-bellied swifts dash across the rocks and bare ground, while brown-shouldered Utes clamber up and down the brush-covered slopes.

During the summer season there are several nature walks each day leaving from the Temple of Sinawava and going about 1 mile up into The Narrows. There are also talks in the evening by Ranger-naturalists on the park's natural features, and a museum at park headquarters.

There is a lodge with separate de luxe cabins open from June 15 to September 10, and a cabin camp that opens in mid-May and continues until October 15. At other times visitors find accommodations at Springdale, just outside the South Entrance.

Zion lies about 315 miles south of Salt Lake City, and 450 east of Los Angeles. Two other national parks are located not too far away. Bryce Canyon is an 86-mile drive to the northeast, while it is about 125 miles due south over the Arizona line to the North Rim of the Grand Canyon, and about twice that distance around to the South Rim. Those who visit Zion and Bryce usually plan to stop also and see Cedar Breaks

128

National Monument. This is a great circle of grotesquely carved cliffs vividly painted in many colors, but in which pink, brown, and orange seem to be most common. It is about midway between the two parks.

HOT SPRINGS

WHEN the ill-fated DeSoto party passed through
what is now Arkansas in the years 1541-42,
they may very well have found the tepees of many
Indians pitched about the cluster of hot springs in the
Ouachita (wash'-ih-taw) Mountains. It is said that the
natives had long known of the mystical properties by
which these waters seemed to cure illness. Tradition
claims that local tribes, even when at war, always
agreed to stop all fighting in the area about these healing springs, which they called "The Land of Peace."

Once owned by France and by Spain, the region
was included in the Louisiana Purchase, and became
a part of the United States in 1803. The next year it
was explored, and in 1807 the first settler built a cabin
in the vicinity. The fame of these many springs and
their strange curative powers spread far and wide, and
numerous pioneer families made long, arduous

journeys so that some member of the family might bathe in their comforting warmth. By 1820, there were enough visitors so that an inn was erected; and ten years later the first bathhouse was opened.

Some even then felt that this great natural wonder should be set aside forever, and freed from selfish control and use. And so it was that in 1832 the hot springs, together with four square miles of surrounding land, were taken over by act of Congress for the future disposal of the United States. The area was known as Hot Springs Reservation, and in 1921, after 89 years, raised to park status, the seventeenth of our natural wonders to be so honored.

There are 47 springs within its boundaries, and they bring to the surface almost a million gallons (or well over 31,000 barrels) of water each day with a temperature of 140° F. It is believed they lie along a "fault line," which is a break reaching down through many layers in the earth's surface, and caused by stress and strain. Rain water sinks in at the surface and continues down a sloping strata of rock until, at a very considerable depth, it comes in contact with a mass of hot rock. It then rises through the break, or "fault line," and in this case appears at the surface as the outflow of the large group of springs. Chemical analyses of each of them show their contents to be almost exactly alike.

Platt National Park in Oklahoma borders the edge of a city. But Hot Springs lies at the very center of a busy metropolis of the same name. The popularity of these healing waters continued to grow as Arkansas filled with people, so the village that sprang up beside this national spa became a town, and finally a flourishing resort city. Today the park embraces several parcels of land which total just over 1000 acres, and spread out onto North, West, Sugar Loaf, and Hot Springs Mountains, and into parts of Indian Mountain and Whittington Parks.

Many people visit the city, and the park within it, to benefit through hydrotherapy, or the treatment of their ailments through the bathing in, or the drinking of, these medicinal waters. For their use there are 18 pay bathhouses, 8 in the park and 10 in the city. All of them are operated under rules and regulations approved by the Secretary of the Interior. There is also a government free bathhouse for the use of those too poor to pay for treatments. The water is also supplied for use in the Army and Navy General Hospital, which is located within the park limits.

The flow from all the springs is collected in a single reservoir, so that identical water is used in each of the bathhouses. Many types of baths are given. Most common is to dip the whole body up to the neck, and let the bather remain in the warm water for about 15 minutes. In other cases it may be in the form of a shower, or perhaps a sitz or sit-down bath, while there are some treatments where only a hand, foot, arm, or leg is immersed in water. In some instances cool water is more beneficial than hot, and specially cooled water is supplied in which there has been no loss of the natural gases. The drinking of the hot, chemically charged water is also considered to be beneficial. So there are several fountains located at convenient points from which visitors may drink water direct from the springs.

The park and the surrounding city of Hot Springs lie almost at the center of the state, and are 50 miles from Little Rock, 190 from Memphis, 290 from Dallas, and a little over 400 from St. Louis. The rugged hill country in which they are located is picturesque, nicely wooded in pine and mixed hardwoods, and has a very temperate climate. Consequently there are many attractions throughout the year. The long fall, brief winter, and the early, lasting spring attract great numbers of visitors from the northern states during that extended period, while summer brings many from points further south. The park is well served with motor roads, and also by an extensive pattern of foot and horseback trails. Roads beyond park boundaries lead out into areas colorful with their examples of Arkansas mountain life.

Hiking within the park is highly rewarding. The forest cover is dense, so that most trails are well shaded; and there are many pleasant spots at which to stop and rest. Several types of park trees bloom attractively, and the autumn foliage is truly beautiful. There are wild-flowers in bloom throughout the year, and while the animal life is somewhat limited, there are nearly 100 species of birds to be seen and heard. The museum in the administration building at the corner of Central and Reserve avenues is well worth visiting. All the various phases of this quite unusual park are explained, and especially the probable way in which the hot springs function.

Only accommodations within park limits are those offered by the public campground in the Gorge, at the foot of Hot Springs Mountain near the eastern boundary. There are fireplaces and tables here, which are used extensively for picnicking, too. But there are large hotels and all other types of tourist facilities in the city of Hot Springs. While it embraces the park, it is run separately, is one of America's foremost resorts, and can be easily reached by railroad, bus, and plane, as well as by private automobile. The neighboring Ouachita upland area is also quite a vacationland, in which a wide variety of adventure awaits the visitor. Here, too, may be found comfortable accommodations to fit any taste and income.

BRYCE CANYON

GRAND, Zion, and Bryce canyons are like three chapters in agelong geological history. The bottom courses in Zion's walls take up the story where it leaves off on the rims of the Grand Canyon. Bryce, in turn, carries on from where the tops of Zion's huge monuments cease. These three canyon parks are grouped near the Utah-Arizona border. Zion is about 80 air miles north of Grand Canyon, while Bryce, by far the youngest of the three, is 25 miles beyond, and a full 40 miles above the Utah border.

Actually Bryce is perhaps better described as an amphitheater than as a canyon. Rain, running water, frost, wind, and other forces have slashed their way down into the Paunsaugunt Plateau. There they have left exposed horseshoe-shaped bowls in its pink and white marly limestone, their walls and faces lined with temples, domes, spires, pinnacles, and other fanciful shapes, stained with all the colors of the rainbow. The Paiute Indians, to whom the area was particularly well known, used to describe it as, "Unka-timpe-wa-wince-pockich," or, as we would say, "red rocks standing like men in a bowl-shaped valley." Indeed much of this lavish display of carving in the gaudy Pink Cliffs formation is so freakish as to seem hardly real.

As in other cases where the rocks worked upon were originally formed from sediment—that is, from small gravel, sand, mud, and limy ooze—they were laid down beneath the waters of some ancient sea. Lime, silica, and iron cemented the particles together, and the weight of overlying strata compressed them into layers of solid rock. Then shifts within the earth's surface thrust them up out of the water, and, in the case of this region, to a height of nearly 2 miles above sea level. As a consequence of this huge lift, the region was split up into enormous blocks many miles along their edges. Then erosion began to break up and wear down these huge rocky masses, cutting deeply into underlying areas. Through the ages many cubic miles of ground-up spoil have been hurried off toward the ocean by dashing streams, capable of much damage and the carrying of heavy loads when in flood.

The edge of one of the great blocks into which this

whole section was split is found in a fault or break that runs through the cliffs of Bryce. There is a noticeable difference in the two halves of the park, marked by the rim of the plateau along the edge of the canyon. West of this line, centuries of erosion have made but little change in the surface. East of it, natural forces have wrought havoc in the softer textured rocks, but have managed to make the series of sculptured amphitheaters places of enchantment. Strangely enough it is not streams pouring down from the top of the little-altered plateau that have slashed their way through hundreds of feet of the Pink Cliffs, and carried billions of tons of refuse to the Colorado River 50 miles to the east. The watercourses on top of the rim flow away in the opposite direction, and have given no aid in these mighty labors. Instead, and it is hard to believe when standing well down toward the bottom of one of the several amphitheaters, these excavations were made solely by rain and snow falling directly into the canyon.

Bryce is about 25 miles east of U.S. 89, and 270 south of Salt Lake City. There is a turnoff from this highway 7 miles south of the town of Panguitch, Utah, and the entrance through Red Canyon often misleads visitors into believing they have already arrived in the park, for this little gorge is extremely colorful. But the larger canyon lies ahead, and is a bit deceptive itself, for it cannot be seen from a distance. In fact it is necessary to stand on its very rim before it suddenly opens up beneath one's feet. The 56 square miles of park area are strung out in a long, irregular block following this outcropping of the Pink Cliffs. There is but a single entrance toward the north end, and some 20 miles of excellent road follows along reasonably close to the rim at the top of the canyon walls, with short spurs in some places to special vantage points. The first of these outlooks is Fairyland, at the head of a canyon of the same name. About 2 miles further on, near park headquarters, is Sunrise Point, overlooking the Queen's Garden. This display lies just to the north of Bryce Canyon itself, and Sunset Point stands at the canyon's head. An inspiring view of this coral and rose-colored abyss can also be had from Inspiration and Bryce points down the rim where it swings to the south and east.

On the opposite side of a bold promontory is Paria View, looking far off to the southeast over Sheep Creek Flat. About 8 miles farther along the main road is Whiteman Cave, the lofty Natural Bridge, and a long vista down over the great work accomplished by the many smaller streams emptying into Willis Creek. But

139

perhaps the most scenic spot of all is Rainbow Point at the road's end near the southern limits of the park. Here there is a sweeping view of about a dozen miles to the northeast that is unforgettable. This highway is open for its full length from April through November, and throughout the year in as far as the headquarters area.

Yet those who limit themselves to the motor road miss much of what the park has to offer. It is necessary to get down off from the high rim to see properly the superb and sometimes grotesque carvings that make the area so remarkable. For this purpose there are excellent horseback and foot trails descending to Silent City, Fairyland, Queen's Garden, Peek-a-boo Canyon, Wall Street, and other distinctive spots. Hiking over them is not too strenuous, and saddle horses, with or without guides, are available.

There is a lodge open during the summer, a cabin camp, and a public campground. Also it is possible to find tourist accommodations along the highways just beyond park limits at all times.

Bryce is operated as a unit together with Zion National Park and Cedar Breaks National Monument. About 35 air miles west of Bryce, but 67 by road, Cedar Breaks is in a manner related to the larger canyon, since both are cut in the same rock formation. Still they are markedly different, for in Cedar Breaks the Pink Cliffs are some 2000 feet deep, and even more highly colored. They are carved with greater massiveness, and without the immense variety of detail found at Bryce. Cedar Breaks's heavily forested rim rises at spots to well above 10,000 feet.

Bryce Canyon, first explored in 1872, was named for a pioneer cattleman. It was proclaimed a monument in 1923, and finally established as a park with its present name in 1928. Cedar Breaks's 6000 acres were made a national monument in 1933.

GRAND TETON

J OHN COLTER, former member of the Lewis and Clark expedition and discoverer of Yellowstone, was undoubtedly the first white man to lay eyes upon the majestic range of mountains but a short distance south of our first national park, in what is now northwestern Wyoming. Soon after his visit in 1807, the Canadian fur traders were penetrating this region, and it was perhaps a French trapper who gave these sharply pointed summits their name of the Grand Tetons. For 15 years, between 1825 and 1840, the Jackson Hole country along Snake River on their eastern flanks was a great gathering place for the "mountain men" hunting beaver pelts.

These close-packed granite spires, which come to a climax in 13,766-foot Grand Teton, form one of the noblest and most arresting ranges in the world. Between its startling scenery and its romantic history, few areas are more deserving of being owned by all the people of the nation. The mountain portion and high country were established as a park in 1929, and in 1943 the Jackson Hole Valley was set aside as a national monument. Then, in 1950, most of the latter was taken into the park, which has become justly popular and one of the most extensively visited areas among the growing number of our public preserves.

Within a distance of 40 miles, the Teton ridge has no less than 20 saw-tooth pinnacles that stab up into the clouds to heights above 10,000 feet. This thickly studded chain of giants is the result of a huge fault or break in the earth's crust. A vast block, many miles long, was thrust up and tilted to the west. Then nature's greedy, restless forces—rain, snow, frost, running water, avalanches, and monstrous glaciers— worked on the huge, rocky uplift and carved it into the area of compelling beauty for the enjoyment of all.

It was the mighty glaciers that chiseled out the angular, pointed peaks and gave a strongly alpine character to all of the high country. They also helped to fashion the Jackson Hole area. Although the term *hole* is widely used in the West to indicate well-closed valleys, it was most fitting in this instance. One of the huge blocks of rocks similar to the Teton Range, but which failed to be pushed up, still lies far out of sight beneath this valley. As the ice rivers gouged cirques, broader canyons, and lake beds on the mountain sides, they also carried the sand, gravel, and boulders down into the deep valley, built it up, and left long moraines, or ridges, of this rubble to serve as dams behind which were formed the very lovely Bradley, Jenny, Leigh, Phelps, Taggart, and Jackson lakes. There are three or four more small jewels in this handsome chain, while above them, high on the shoulders of the range, are countless other gemlike mountain tarns.

The nearly 470 square miles within park boundaries make this still big-game country. Here is the home of one of the largest herds of elk in all the world. These wapiti, as the Indians called these great, reddish brown deer, move up into the high country as the snow melts, and back to lower ranges with the late fall snows. Legal hunting now has to be encouraged to keep the herd from increasing in numbers beyond the grazing capacity of the winter pastures. It now numbers between 16,000 and 20,000.

More commonly seen, however, is the far less wary moose, biggest member of the deer family, which feeds in the ponds and slews. Mule deer are on the increase, but they tend to be somewhat shy in this park, and are seen mostly out along the trails. Bears also prefer to keep to the higher country, as do the limited herds of Rocky Mountain bighorn sheep. There are considerable quantities of smaller animals from chipmunks to coyotes, and more than 100 species of birds. Largest among the latter is the bald eagle, whose nest may be 5 feet across and equally thick, containing as much as 200 or more pounds of branches and twigs.

One of Grand Teton's most remarkable exhibits is seldom seen, for far too few of its visitors care to make the effort to reach it. It is the "cloud gardens," the alpine regions reached only by means of a pack trip up into the high country. The floral decorations on the shoulders of the mountains are both gorgeous and unique. Many species thrive best at elevations between 10,000 and 12,000 feet, and their variety here on top of the world seems to be virtually endless. A good example is the blue, starry-eyed sky pilot, unhappily also called skunk flower because its crushed leaves have so unsavory an odor. The pink-belled mountain heath flourishes where the air is thin and the moisture scarce. Yet the vivid, persistent paintbrush will grow from the lowlands all the way up to cloud-parting summits. Especially warm and cheering on these chilly heights are the blooms that run to yellow and gold. Outstanding among them are the glacier lilies, columbines, ranunculuses, alpine sunflowers, and arnicas. The range has formed a barrier to plant migration, and certain species found on its slopes have never passed beyond the summits. The blooming season begins as the snows melt from the upland meadows in May, and continues through August. The timber cover is mostly evergreen, with some aspen, alder, and cottonwood about water holes and stream courses. These latter trees grow very colorful with the first fall frost.

U.S. Routes 26, 89, 187, and 287 pass through various sections of the park, and together with secondary roads reach most points of interest in the lowlands. The trail system, still being extended, serves both the lake chain at the west edge of Jackson Hole and Snake River Valley, and also large stretches of the high country between Paintbrush and Death canyons. The trails can be attacked either on foot or on horseback, and saddle and pack animals, together with skilled guides, are available.

To some the stern, rugged peaks themselves are a clear challenge. But while mountain climbing is permitted, it is hedged with certain restrictions. Teton peaks can be very hazardous, and the inexperienced may encounter serious mishaps and even loss of life.

146

Authorized guides are available, and all parties must register at the beginning of the climb and also report its completion.

There is barely a 5-mile break between the northern boundary of Grand Teton and the southern limits of Yellowstone, although it is 142 miles between the two headquarters. It is about 285 miles south to Salt Lake City, and some 460 across the state to Cheyenne. The park can be reached by rail, bus, and plane, although the great majority arrive by automobile. Highways from the east, south, and west are kept open throughout the year. U.S. 89, running down from Yellowstone and the north, is snowed in during the winter, and not cleared for traffic until late May. The park season is principally from June 15 to September 15, and there is a variety of places to stay overnight at several points within its bounds, including lodges, dude ranches, and three well-developed campgrounds at Jenny, String, and Jackson lakes. Finest of all is the recently built $6,000,000 Jackson Lake Lodge, erected by John D. Rockefeller, Jr., which offers superb accommodations to some 1100 guests on a non-profit basis. Its lobby window, 26 feet high and 60 feet long, permits one of the finest views of the park.

Even the summers can be crisp at times, and sudden

snowstorms blow down from the high country occasionally in June and July. But in the cold months this is truly a winter wonderland, and Jackson Hole has become famous for winter sports. These center about the town of Jackson, and the one- and three-mile ski runs on neighboring Snow King Mountain, where there is a chair lift. There are also exciting cross-country ski tours, and ample, crisp snow on which to enjoy them from November to May.

GREAT SMOKY MOUNTAINS

Long before the towering Rocky Mountains had been thrust up from the ocean bottom, the many ranges of the Appalachian Mountain system stretched north and south through the eastern half of North America. This great upland had been formed at one of the most violent points in the earth's long history, but has been worn down and greatly smoothed and rounded by almost endless erosion. One of its highest ranges is the Great Smokies, so named because of the deep blue, smokelike haze which so often hangs above its summits. They form one of the oldest highland chains upon earth, and are most massive where they form the boundary between North Carolina and Tennessee. There, along one 36-mile stretch, the land does not fall at a single point below 5000 feet, and 16 peaks rise above 6000 feet.

While a relatively few hardy pioneers explored and

settled in this and neighboring mountain fastnesses, the area was long isolated and little visited from the outside. It had splendid forests, some sections of which were logged, and the few that did penetrate this vast wilderness told arresting stories of its majestic beauty. As paved highways crept higher and higher into the hills, the feeling increased that here was an area well worth preserving. A park was authorized by Congress as early as 1926, providing there were sufficient donations of land to the federal government. The two states within whose borders it would lie began to acquire territory, and substantial funds were also contributed by John D. Rockefeller, Jr., in memory of his mother. Deeds to just over 156,000 acres were turned over to the Secretary of the Interior early in 1930, and the Park Service took charge of this limited park. It was formally dedicated in 1940, and the tract has now grown to over a half million acres.

From Chilhowee, Tennessee, to Cataloochee, North Carolina, the east-west length of the park is just a trifle over 50 air miles, while there are several points where it runs 18 or 19 miles wide. The crest of the Great Smoky ridge zigzags for some 74 miles through the preserve. This forms the boundary between the two states, and is also the pathway for the famous Appalachian Trail from Maine to Georgia. It weaves its way over the shoulders of many "summits," "tops," and "balds" in the 50 air miles from Davenport Gap to Doe Knob at heights above 5000 feet. There it drops down to cross the Little Tennessee River by way of Fontana Dam.

The Cherokee Indians were the original "mountaineers" inhabiting these highlands. They still continue to live in their reservation which borders the park at the southeast. They were followed by settlers largely of English and Scottish origin who sought to farm the steep mountainsides, and produced a primitive but colorful culture. A display of original buildings, cabins, barns, and a working, water-powered grist mill may be seen at the end of the improved road at Cades Cove, 26 miles west of Gatlinburg Entrance. There is a similar display, together with a Pioneer Museum, 2 miles inside the Cherokee Entrance in North Carolina.

Visitors may travel over 66 miles of high standard roads within the park. Yet it is claimed that only about 5 per cent of its area and real wonders can be seen from this highway. It does reach to the top of Clingmans Dome, third highest point east of the Mississippi, and there are many turnouts along it, notably the one at 5048-foot Newfound Gap, where there are magnificent views. There are 77 more miles of secondary roads, which reach out into highly scenic areas. But those who wish to see the beauties of the sections which are still absolute wilderness must depend upon the 650 odd miles of saddle and foot trails. Some of these are bridle paths, others improved footpaths, and some merely tracks through the dense forest growth. They vary from easy, pleasant stretches to some very strenuous trails suitable only for the most experienced hikers. Riding and pack animals, together with experienced guides, are available at points outside of but bordering the reservation.

One of the great wonders of the park is its marvelous plant life. The forest growth is the finest in the eastern United States, with a surprising variety of trees, both evergreens and hardwoods, totaling no less than 130 species in all. Between a third and a half of this vast domain is virgin forest, where timber has never been felled.

Beside the many trees the great assortment of shrubs, herbs, and other plant forms makes this a botanist's paradise. The great beauty of its wildflowers, too, can be readily appreciated by all. There is bloom from late February until the witchhazel finally sheds its clusters of yellow blossoms in December. The dogwood and other spring flowers are a sight to behold in the last two weeks of April. But the exhibits that bring hosts of visitors are those presented by the mountain laurel, the flame azalea, and the purple and later white rhododendron.

The annual rainfall, which averages about 100 inches, makes the vegetation very lush. The laurel and rhododendron especially react to this abundant moisture, and grow in huge patches known locally as "slicks" or "woolly heads." These shrubs sometimes attain tree size and form perfect jungles, which are favorite haunts of the park's many bears. The laurel colors the hillsides during May and early June, after which the flame azaleas and rose-purple rhododendrons take over. The latter carry over into July, particularly at higher altitudes, by which time the white rhododendrons begin their bloom, and are generally at their best about the middle of the month.

Another period of brilliant color comes in the fall, when the many trees that shed their leaves are decked in reds and golds that blend so nicely with the deep green of the spruces, firs, and hemlocks. Many who drive across the park over U.S. 441 during the colder months find interest in the heavy beards of frost on tree branches on some of the higher spurs, left by moisture-laden clouds dragging across this mighty upland.

While the summer days may be hot, and gray mists swirl up out of valleys to billow about the summits, the nights are always cool. Spring comes early at the lower levels, and follows rather rapidly up into the high country. Fall days are especially lovely, with dry, clear air which makes the longer views very impressive. There are rainy and foggy days during the winter, with infrequent snows, and roads may be iced at times from sleet and frozen moisture. The park is open throughout the year.

Its wildlife will be encountered along the trails, while fishing the 600 miles of trout streams. There are 52 species of fur-bearing animals, among them the black bear, white-tailed deer, red and gray foxes, and many other creatures. The more than 200 types of birds include the handsome ruffed grouse, and especially the wild turkey, which is increasing in this sanctuary.

The one overnight lodge within the park is atop 6593-foot Mount LeConte, and is reached only on foot or horseback. There are campgrounds on the Tennessee side at Chimney Tops and Cades Cove; and also across the mountains in North Carolina at Smokemont and

Deep Creek. However, many hotels, motels, and other facilities will be found in the cities and towns just beyond park borders.

There are two entrances in Tennessee. One is at Townsend, 29 miles from Knoxville, and 125 from Chattanooga. The other is just beyond the resort town of Gatlinburg, 40 miles from Knoxville. The Cherokee Entrance in North Carolina is 47 miles from Asheville, and about 190 miles from Atlanta, Georgia. The 477-mile Blue Ridge Parkway, under Park Service direction, connects Great Smoky Mountains with Shenandoah National Park in Virginia. Located close to the geographical center of the eastern half of the country, this mountain fastness draws the most visitors of any of our national parks.

CARLSBAD CAVERNS

THE special features which attract visitors to three of our national parks are concealed beneath the earth's surface, and in each instance the discovery of these hidden wonders was a bit unusual. It was a wounded bear that led a hunter into Mammoth Cave. Another hunter felt a strange blast of air blowing from a small hole in the earth, and Wind Cave became known. But mighty Carlsbad Caverns in southeastern New Mexico had a far more unique way of letting early cattlemen know of its huge underground passages. Each evening during the summer millions of bats make their way out through the cave entrance and fly off in search of night-flying insects. So great are the numbers of these uncouth, winged creatures—estimates vary from 5,000,000 to 8,000,000 in a good season—that they sometimes take up to four hours to clear the exit. As day begins to dawn they start to return, and affix themselves to the ceiling of Bat Cave, often as many as 300 occupying a space no more than one foot square. Naturalists have counted as many as 14 species of these small winged mammals.

The Indians knew of this immense cave, as the remains of camps about its entrance and crude paintings on the entrance walls well testify. Early pioneers may have been in the vicinity, but this semidesert region was little known until the cowboys and miners began to move in during the 1880s. The upper portions of the cave were soon explored, and first interest in it was the mining and removal of thousands of tons of bat guano, a valuable fertilizer, at first stacked almost to the ceiling of the Bat Cave section.

Jim White, a local boy who had worked with these miners, became very interested in the other parts of this subterranean miracle. He came to know it very well, and often guided parties into its depths. Its fame slowly grew, and in 1923 it was proclaimed a national monument. Fortunately the National Geographic Society made extensive explorations during 1923-24, and the nationwide publicity that resulted brought hosts of visitors. By 1930 its popularity warranted its being established as Carlsbad Caverns National Park. In the meanwhile Jim White had become a ranger, and finally was appointed chief ranger in the region he knew so well.

The park, which has been extended to include about 46,000 acres, lies just off U.S. Routes 62 and 180. It is 27 miles south of the city of Carlsbad, and about 160 east and north of El Paso. Rail and plane connections can be made at either of these places. While there are no overnight accommodations within the park—and no campground—hotels, motels, and other facilities are available at Carlsbad and along the highway. A visit is customarily limited to a single day, since the conducted tour underground is completed in about 4 hours.

This cavern, as was true in the case of Mammoth and Wind Caves, resulted from underground water dissolving and carrying away untold quantities of material from two rock formations. These are the Tansill and the Capitan limestones, lying well beneath the surface. Great quantities of oxygen-rich water worked upon them, and small cracks and crevices slowly became larger, and finally ended up as mile upon mile of lofty, spacious chambers and twisting, turning, connecting passageways. Then came the long period when these tremendous voids received their lavish decoration. A bewildering array of ornaments hangs from the

Union Pacific Railroad Photo

Above: The jagged Tetons form a glorious backdrop to lovely Jackson Lake, largest of several thrilling lakes scattered in the foothills of Grand Teton National Park. *Below:* For thirty-six miles along their main crest the Great Smoky Mountains rise in excess of 5000 feet. More people visit this park than any other of our twenty-nine national parks.

Photo by W. Ray Scott—National Park Concessions, Inc.

MILE HIGH

GREAT SMOKY MOUNTAINS NATIONAL PARK
RIDGE IS THE N. CAR. - TENN. STATE LINE

Above: Shenandoah's trail system leads through a wonderland of wooded ridges and glades, and beside tranquil streams and dashing waterfalls set amid the most beautiful scenery. *Below left:* The Rock of Ages in Carlsbad Caverns National Park, huge underground wonderland. *Below right:* Temple of the Sun, a feature in the Big Room 750 feet below ground at Carlsbad.

Photos by W. Ray Scott–National Park Concessions, Inc.

Above: In Mammoth Cave, as at Carlsbad Caverns, lunch is served underground to visitors. Snowball Dining Room gets its name from the crystal gypsum clusters on the roof.   *Left:* Frozen Niagara is the largest travertine, or onyx, deposit of many in Mammoth Cave. It takes most of a day for even a quick view of this cave's many, many wonders.

National Park Service Photo

Above: Deer Park on the eastern edge of Olympic National Park is a favorite skiing spot. The snowfall here, while ample, is far lighter than west of these mountains. *Right:* Trees of enormous size grow in a junglelike rain forest in the western part of Olympic National Park. The ranger gives an idea of how large trees can become.

Western Ways Photo

ceilings. Many are like icicles, and many, too, look like growing plants. Springing up from the floors are the cone- and column-like stalagmites, and in this cave the far rarer twisted and branched formations known as helictites. Because of the vast size of some of the rooms and the great height of their ceilings, the ornamentation is massive, in keeping with their magnitude.

While there are well over 20 miles of explored passages, and quite likely many more of yet unvisited corridors and chambers, the complete tour requires only 2¾ miles of walking. It begins at the sole natural entrance, and swings away from the passage leading to Bat Cave into an immense Auditorium. Here the tour leader addresses his party and explains, among other things, that they are about to begin a sharp descent of more than 800 feet. Once there was flight after flight of stairs. Now the paved trails slope down a series of switchbacks. Yet they can be rather hard on leg muscles, for some stretches are like the steepest mountain paths.

The first real spectacle is the Main Corridor, a mighty tunnel sculptured like a cathedral, and a mile long. It plunges down about 500 feet in that distance, during which the visitor passes Devil's Spring, Whale's Mouth, the American Eagle, the Baby Hippo, and the

Three Little Monkeys. But the cavern's real beauty lies ahead, and is quickly found in the first cluster of chambers, which includes the Green Lake Room, King's Palace, Queen's Chamber, and the tiny Papoose Room. The short, steep climb up out of the King's Palace and around past the Boneyard is quite fittingly called Appetite Hill. It not only helps to build an appetite, but also to satisfy it, for the trail soon forks, and a left turn takes one through a passage to the lunchroom.

Here visitors queue up, pick up a box lunch and something to drink, and find a vacant place at one of the host of white picnic tables. A pause of 40 minutes is provided in which to eat an unhurried lunch, and to give eyes and legs a well-earned rest. This is all done no less than 754 feet below the surface of the park, and there is ample room for some 2000 other visitors to refresh themselves in this remarkable lunchroom each hour.

Returning to the main trail, the guided parties move on past Rock of Ages, the best-known formation of all, located in the famous Big Room, largest of all the caverns. So vast is it that the trail circling its edges is 1¼ miles long. At one point the ceiling is 285 feet above the floor. Yet because of its irregular shape, it is hard to believe that it is a single room. However, it is possible to draw a straight line nearly 1800 feet long in one direction through it, and about 900 in another. Its decorations run all the way from tiny, needlelike formations to the great domes that stand near its entrance in the Hall of Giants. The largest of them towers more than 60 feet above the edge of the trail. Thousands of lance-pointed stalactites hang threateningly from the Big Room's roof. Yet it is claimed that no rock has fallen within the cave for thousands of years.

The tours, always in charge of a leader, leave at regular intervals during the morning and early afternoon. While the second half, involving the Big Room and a brief look into the lower, unvisited cave at the Jumping-off Place, is easier, most are ready to quit at the end of 4 hours. Even on warm days outside, the 56° temperature in the cave sometimes seems a trifle cool, especially when stops are made for brief lectures by the guide. But cool as it may be, it is comforting to know that the trip back out of the caverns does not have to be made on foot. Near the restaurant is a bank of elevators. These bring many down to the more interesting level, and take all visitors back to the surface. They are capable of carrying 1200 people each hour.

The principal feature in the park above ground is

the evening flight of the bats. This takes place only during the summer months, for as soon as the night-flying insects begin to depart with the onset of cooler weather, the bats migrate into Mexico in search of continuing food supply. Many who know of this unusual daily occurrence time their visit so it may be seen. A naturalist assembles those interested at the cave entrance a short time before the exodus begins, and gives a brief talk on the bats and their habits.

SHENANDOAH

THE Blue Ridge Mountains have won great fame in song and story for their stately beauty and their romantic and historic associations. In Virginia the lofty ridge lies to the east of the glorious Shenandoah Valley. In earlier days this area was our very first "West," and something of a "Wild West," too, as settlers pushed pack trains and then wagons down this valley trailway to find homes along the Piedmont Plateau stretching from central Pennsylvania into northern Georgia. One of the first to penetrate the area with high purpose was Governor Spotswood of Virginia. In 1716 he and a party of the province's principal men— his Knights of the Golden Horseshoe—crossed over into the huge north-south valley through a pass now called Swift Run Gap. Today Spotswood Trail, or U.S. 33, finds its way across the southern half of Shenandoah National Park at this same opening through the hills.

Sixty-five miles to the north, at Front Royal, the range begins to mount rapidly. Its peaks are soon up around the 4000-foot level, and find their highest point in 4049-foot Hawksbill Mountain. Yet they are not jagged, glacier-cut mountains, but rather imposing, friendly highlands, further softened as a rule by the faint bluish haze that gives them their name. Forested up to their summits, they were rather rugged for extensive settlement, and were long admired from afar rather than extensively visited. Yet by the 1920s there was agitation to include this region in a national park. Interest grew, and in 1935 friends of the scheme presented the federal government with deeds to 176,430 acres. The park was dedicated the next year, and has grown somewhat until it now embraces about 300 square miles.

It is 104 miles between the North and South Entrance Stations, as measured over the course of the famous Skyline Drive that runs its entire length along the crest of the ridge. This excellent motor road begins at an elevation of 705 feet, achieves a maximum of 3680 at Skyland, and for 87 miles is above 2000 feet. The 2028-mile Appalachian Trail parallels this motor road almost from one entrance to the other. The long, irregular preserve is not much above 8 miles wide at any point, and often but half that width. It is cut into three nearly equal sections by Lee Highway, or U.S. 211, which climbs over the ridge through Thornton Gap, and also by Spotswood Highway mentioned above. There are entrance stations at both points where these east-west roads cross Skyline Drive. Thus there is ready access to all portions of the park.

One of the great sports enjoyed there is hiking, and in addition to the 94-mile section of the graded Appalachian Trail there are foot and pack trails to mountaintops, cliffs, waterfalls, and other scenic features throughout the park. Any who prefer to go by horseback may rent saddle and pack animals at Skyland during the summer and fall. For those making overnight trips, there are closed, trailside cabins complete with bunks, bedding, cooking equipment, and other facilities, available through the Trail Club. There are also three-sided trailside shelters, with bunks and an outdoor fireplace, for the use of all on a first-come-first-served basis. They must be shared up to their full capacity. This bit of trail etiquette also calls up another—each group of occupants should leave a clean cabin and surroundings, and a supply of dry wood, if possible, well back in the shelter. Fires can be built only in provided fireplaces, unless a permit for open

165

campfires has been issued by one of the park rangers.

Nature has been most bountiful along this superb ridge of mountains. It is almost entirely woodland, the chief tree being the oak. Visitors also find hickories, locusts, gums, American chestnuts, maples, lindens, and walnuts. There are numerous stream courses, and along them are birches, tulip trees, sycamores, and elms. Evergreens within the park are divided between pines, spruces, hemlocks, cedars, firs, and yews; they appear to be more extensive in the south end of the park, where the soil is much drier, since they grow to full size, while the hardwood growth tends to be dwarfed. Several of the latter, including the cherry, redbud, dogwood, locust, chestnut, and tulip, bloom attractively during the spring. And they, together with the other trees that shed their leaves, paint the mountainsides with glowing colors in mid-October. This riotous display brings great numbers to the park area.

The shrubs also make their own fine contribution. The azalea, joined by the wild crabapple and the hawthorn, attract many visitors in May. As that month moves along into June, the mountain laurel is particularly handsome, while the Jersey-tea, ninebark, and sumac bloom prettily in midsummer. But the park would be far less bright and appealing without its abundance of wildflowers. There are many, many kinds, and some that are quite rare.

While there are 40 species of mammals, they are mostly the smaller creatures, although there are fair-sized herds of white-tailed deer, and increasing numbers of black bears. More than 200 kinds of birds have been seen, some of them very colorful, and others, like the wild turkey, extremely scarce. There are many box and snapping turtles, and at least two poisonous snakes, the timber rattlesnake and the copperhead. These latter, however, are almost never found along the trails.

There is a lodge at Big Meadows, and cabins for overnight guests at a number of points, which are available during the summer and fall. There is also a wide variety of accommodations for visitors along the highways that parallel and cross through the park. In addition to cabins and shelters along the trails, there is a tent and trailer campground at the Big Meadows Wayside. Picnickers will find tables and other conveniences at several inviting points along the Skyline.

The park is open throughout the year, although the Skyline may be closed to traffic briefly because of fog or clouds, and while being cleared of snow. Winters are bringing an increasing number of visitors to the park, for some sections provide excellent skiing during the colder months. It is about 80 miles from Washington to the North Entrance, or 95 to the entrance from U.S. 211 at Thornton Gap. South Entrance is about the same distance from Richmond, and 90 miles from Roanoke. Shenandoah is connected with Great Smoky Mountains National Park by the 477-mile Blue Ridge Parkway, which is under the direction of the Park Service.

MAMMOTH CAVE

ONE day in 1799 a pioneer, named Houchin, was hunting bear in southern Kentucky, about 30 miles across the hills from the Sinking Spring beside which Abraham Lincoln would be born ten years later. Having wounded one of the "critters," he took off in pursuit, only to have it disappear into the darkness of a cave. A bear had been lost, but another of the large caves which abound in this region had been discovered. But this one was to prove over the years to be the second largest cavern in the world, exceeded only by Carlsbad Caverns in New Mexico. Soon people were prying into its secrets, and over 150 miles of its passageways, rooms, and underground lakes and rivers have now been explored.

It all began about 240,000,000 years ago when a huge bed of limestone was laid down beneath the waters of a vast arm of the ocean. Slowly these stratas of rock were raised above sea level, and then rain water went to work. Seeping through to the limestone, it dissolved and honeycombed the mass, carrying away tons upon tons of the dissolved rock and leaving great mazes of corridors, lofty openings like great rooms, and other empty spaces. This was the first and very necessary step in cave formation. But without their customary decoration, these great voids would be barren indeed. As water continues to seep through roofs and walls, it often bears other dissolved rock and minerals in liquid form. It is thus dripstone, and deposits its burden as iciclelike stalactites, hanging from the ceiling, and columnlike stalagmites, building up from the floor. Sometimes the water acts as flowstone, coating the walls with wavy draperies, or giving the floor a glasslike finish. Gypsum in the water can deck ceilings with woolly masses, or with strange pendants and flowerlike growths. Certain other dissolved chemicals add brilliant colors to such decorative work.

In the Mammoth Cave the cavernous corridors occur at five separate levels. It was finally found that the reason for this lay outside the cavern itself. The Green River, which flows through the 80 square miles of the park preserve, had slowly cut its way lower and lower into the earth. Since it controlled the drainage of water from the cave, and had for long periods flowed at certain levels, there were five distinct "floors" in the cavern. The lowest of these is about 350 feet below ground surface.

There are four principal entrances, the natural one, into which the bear escaped, and through which the Indians used to make their way, for they seem to have made some use of the cave, as mummies, tools, and other objects left by them bear witness. The other major openings are man-made, and are known as Frozen Niagara, New, and Carmichael Entrances. Several different guided trips below ground are provided, taking from 1 or 1½ hours to as long as 7½ hours. Those who take the longer tours stop for refreshments in the Snowball Dining Room, the ceiling of which is covered with fluffy ovals of gypsum crystals. A drinking-water fountain here supplies water from an upside-down well. The names of some of the points which may be visited are quite interesting. They include Bottomless Pit, Fat Man's Misery, Echo Dome, Giant's Coffin, Martha Washington's Statue, Grand Central Station, Kentucky Avenue, Dead Sea, and the Minnehaha Islands.

Most mysterious of them all perhaps is Echo River. It is on the fifth or lowest level, more than 100 yards

171

below the entrances. It varies from 20 to 60 feet wide, and from 10 to 30 feet deep. Only a small portion of its course has been explored, due to the lowness of the roof at many points. However, boat trips over a portion of its course are a part of the longer tours. Its level is controlled by that of the Green River, and when that stream is in flood the water of submerged Echo River completely fills the cavity through which it flows. Blind fish swim in its waters, and blind insects fly above them, for natural light has never found its way into this giant cavity far within the earth. Crystal Lake, on which there are short boat trips, is 270 feet underground.

But the park has many features upon its surface to attract visitors. The rolling countryside is nicely forested, principally with hardwoods, and a sprinkling of evergreens. The hillsides are bright with dogwood and redbud in April and May, and with mountain laurel just a few weeks later. In October the autumn colors are especially beautiful when seen from the high lookout towers. There are herds of deer and quite a variety of smaller wildlife, including some 170 species of birds.

Those who enjoy hiking and trees, flowers, and wildlife will find real pleasure in the trails that wind through the woods along the bluffs beside the Green River. There are excursion boat trips on this lovely stream, and fishing in it and in the smaller Nolin River at the western edge of the park. A free camp-ground and a picnic ground are available, with tables, fireplaces, wood for fuel, comfort stations, and a laundry and shower facilities with running water. There is also a section for automobile trailers.

The park is 11 miles west of Cave City located on U.S. 31W and is about 100 miles south of Louisville and an equal distance north of Nashville. It is just over 200 miles to either Cincinnati or Knoxville. The improved road, State Route 70, runs in only as far as the facilities near the entrance to the cave. Access to all other sections within the boundaries is by unim-proved roads or trails.

The Mammoth Cave Hotel is open all year, al-though outlying cottages and cabins are available only during the summer season. Many depend upon the extensive tourist accommodations found along the main highway a few miles to the east.

While the cave saw use as a source of saltpeter for gunpowder during the War of 1812, and was long visited as a natural wonder, it was not until 1926 that Congress authorized the establishment of Mammoth

Cave National Park. There was a provision in this act that the necessary land, which had long been privately owned, would be donated to the federal government. The people of Kentucky, with some assistance from federal sources, acquired the essential area, and the park became fully established in 1941.

OLYMPIC

THE northwestern tip of the United States—the Olympic Peninsula in the state of Washington—is the wettest spot in the entire country. This is especially true of its Pacific slopes, where it is quite normal for more than 12 feet of rain to fall within a year. Centuries of such wetness have developed a rain forest which is one of the chief features, and surely the most unique, of Olympic National Park.

But it was actually the rugged, snow- and glacier-covered Olympic Mountains, lying east of the rain forest, that first drew attention to this region. Rising, as some of its peaks do, almost from sea level, this ridge looks very massive when viewed from the Juan de Fuca Strait or the Puget Sound country. Spanish and British sea captains had seen and recorded these picturesque highlands long before Americans had found their way into the area. In fact a Britisher named its crowning peak, "Mount Olympus," in 1788.

It was not until 1846 that the Northwest became a part of the United States, and more than 40 years later before the interior of the Olympic Peninsula received much serious attention. An expedition crossed from north to south in 1889-90 and brought out word of the many natural wonders there. It was felt that the region deserved government protection, and in 1897 a portion of the peninsula was set aside as a national forest. Twelve years later some 960 square miles were proclaimed a national monument, which became a park in 1938. With the additional territory added in 1953, it now ranks fifth in size among the areas that have achieved that status.

The rain forest, which can be reached by road in the valleys of the Hoh, Queets, and Quinault rivers, is a dank, eerie, primeval wilderness. The chief trees are the Sitka spruces and western hemlocks, with somewhat fewer numbers of Douglas firs and western red cedars. Still the largest known example of each of these four spices grows within the park, and there are countless specimens of all four kinds more than 8 feet through at the butt, and which stand more than 200 feet tall at their topmost branches.

In addition to these big trees there is a far smaller moss-covered vine maple that grows beneath the huge evergreens. A deep carpet of moss is spread over the forest floor, and soon hides fallen tree trunks and climbs up the stems of those still standing. Another variety, a club moss, is draped and festooned on tree branches. Ferns grow among these mosses both on the ground and well up into the limbs of the trees. Although it may sound dark and grim, yet on pleasant days this forest glows with a pleasing, greenish light. Big-leaf maples, alders, and cottonwoods are found along its watercourses.

The firs and the hemlocks push up the slopes above the rain forest, are joined for a time by other evergreens, and continue the woodland cover up to the timber line at about 5500 feet. The alpine meadows at this point and above are filled with wildflowers, which bloom from June through October. The mountain types are particularly abundant in the Hurricane Ridge section in the northeast corner of the park, although there are sufficient varieties so that there is bloom throughout the park.

With its 888,000 acres, this great preserve is, of course, an outstanding wildlife refuge. Outstanding, too, is its herd of 4000 or more Olympic elk, also called the Roosevelt elk. Millions have enjoyed the excellent motion picture Walt Disney made of the life story of this handsome beast, which may be seen alive in the park. Some remain in the lowlands at all times. But the majority follow melting snows up into their "home" valleys to summer in the high country. The black-tailed deer also migrate, but can often be seen in the meadows during their morning and evening feeding periods. The black bears are most frequently encountered in the upland meadows; and there are more than 50 other species of wild animals within park limits. They are scattered all the way from the ocean-front beaches, through the rain and higher forests and the alpine meadows, up to the snow-covered peaks. In these varied life zones there are also about 140 types of birds.

No one can visit Olympus without being captivated by its mountains. The Olympic Range was thrust up for the third and last time about 5,000,000 years ago, at about the time the volcanic Cascade Range was also being formed. Their present ruggedness is due to the heavy erosion they have had to withstand. Where 12 feet of rain falls lower down in the rain forest, the high country on the western side receives the equivalent of almost half again that amount of moisture, principally as snow. This great burden does not all melt, but gathers as glaciers, which over many thousands of years have worn down the height of these mountains and left them sharp and jagged. Mount Olympus, the highest peak, is 7954 feet. Several others top 7000 feet, while much of the crest of the ridges and peaks is close to 6000.

Where once these summits were being scored by a glacial ice sheet 3000 feet thick, this grinding, tearing blanket has long since disappeared. Yet there are still no less than 50 glaciers in these mountains, covering in all an area of nearly 30 square miles. They are now relatively small. Still the three largest of the six ice rivers on the shoulders of Mount Olympus are 2 or more miles in length. And they are still scouring the sides of these peaks just as they have been for thousands of years. Those interested in seeing glaciers at first hand in this park should look to Mounts Anderson, Tom, Christie, and Carrie, in addition to Mount Olympus.

U.S. Route 101, which originates in the city of Olympia, circles the park on three sides before heading south through Hoquiam and Aberdeen, and then continues on down the Pacific shore line to the Mexican border. This highway passes through the park for about 12 miles at each of two points. It contacts the resort areas at Lake Crescent, the Ocean Strip, and about

Lake Quinault. There are secondary roads running in at many points to other resort areas and public campgrounds. These also make connection with the more than 500 miles of hiking and pack trails. There are many interesting trips that can be made on foot, lasting from an hour or two to several weeks, and there is mountain climbing for those who are experienced. Horses and guides can be rented for both short or long trips.

The fishing is excellent, not only in the park, but also in both fresh and salt water areas close by. Streams and lakes within the boundaries contain eastern brook, cutthroat, Dolly Varden, rainbow, and steelhead trout. Salmon can be caught in the salt water that borders this great preserve on three sides.

While Olympic National Park receives visitors all the year, the most popular season is summer and early fall. By July most of the trails, even those in the high country, are free from snow, and the weather by then is mostly sunny but pleasantly cool. The bright, brisk fall days of September and October are specially delightful. There are extensive overnight accommodations both in the park and along nearby highways. The road to Deer Park Lodge, in the extreme northeast corner of the park, is open all winter to the ski runs there, which are much sought on weekends and holidays between Christmas time and the end of March.

This is a most appropriate point at which to mention the constant watchfulness the National Park Service must exercise lest our fine heritage in the parks be spoiled or lost. Sometimes suggestions for changes within them are well meant but wholly unsuitable, yet they may be backed by groups which are able to bring great pressure to bear. In the case of Olympic National Park, much effort has been expended by very selfish interests claiming that the park is too big, when it appears that the intent is primarily to gain possession of a part of this area for private gain.

ISLE ROYALE

ONE of the last established of our twenty-nine national parks has several very unique features. There are no roads and not a single wheeled vehicle within its 210 square miles. It is actually closer to a foreign land than it is to United States territory. And some of the creatures which now live in this forested wilderness found their way within its boundaries across 15 miles of water, in fairly recent times. This unusual region is Isle Royale, largest island in Lake Superior, lying in the northern portion of the lake near the point where Minnesota meets the province of Ontario.

This huge splinter of land, 45 miles long and 9 miles in its greatest width, was left well above its surroundings when the huge glaciers, which once spread over the northern half of the continent, scooped out the depressions now filled by the waters of Superior

182

and the other Great Lakes. Its billion-year-old rocks are very much like those in the copper-rich Keweenah Peninsula in upper Michigan, some 45 miles across the water to the southeast. For thousands of years it was submerged. Then, as the level of the Great Lakes lowered, it was thrust out into the open until its highest point, Ishpeming Point, now stands 705 feet above the lake surface. It is actually an archipelago, made up of the large, main island and some 200 minor islets and neighboring rocks.

It was early known to the French of Canada, for it stood not far offshore at the entrance to the Grand Portage in Minnesota, which gave access to the waterways penetrating the lake country and the Northwest. It is called *Minong* on their early maps, and later renamed in honor of King Louis XIV.

But the Indians had known it well centuries earlier, for they had gathered its free copper, and carried on very primitive mining and smelting operations at hundreds of points on its shores and hillsides, long before Columbus crossed the ocean. Roasting copper-bearing rocks in roaring fires, they then dashed them with cold lake water to crack the larger chunks so they could be crushed into small bits with hammerstones. Articles made from this Isle Royale copper have been found among remains left by Indians that lived far down in what are now our southeastern States, and also at scattered points across the Great Plains.

The island seems to have been trapped by the French *voyageurs* seeking hides for the American Fur Company, and for a time in the early 1800s this concern also operated fisheries from three of its harbors. However, Isle Royale was actually Indian territory until the Chippewas ceded it back to the United States in 1843. Quickly it was overrun by prospectors, certain the traces of crude mining left by the early red men would lead them to great wealth. For more than 50 years exploration and mining operations gripped this secluded island. Some ore was recovered, and one huge specimen weighing close to 3 tons was hauled all the way to Philadelphia for the Centennial Exhibition in 1876. Yet most of this great effort showed poor returns, and in 1899 the last mine was abandoned. Quickly this peaceful land began to return to a *state of nature*.

In 1931 Congress authorized the establishment of Isle Royale and the surrounding islands, some of which are 2 or more miles in length, as a national park. But it was 1940 before all parcels of privately owned land had been acquired, and 1946 before the area was formally dedicated.

Another unique feature of this island fastness results from its location. It combines the hardwood forests of the upper tiers of states with the northern forest typical of Canada. Such trees as the sugar maple and yellow birch, which are very common at the southwestern end of the big island from Lake Desor to Washington Harbor, are at the northern limit of their growth. The upper three quarters of Isle Royale is covered with balsam firs, spruces, poplars, and white birches common to the boreal forests of Canada. Since prospectors often burned off the forest cover to make it easier to find rock outcroppings, there are perhaps a greater number of birches and poplars than usual, for they tend to grow first on burned-over land.

This is extremely cold country, and the growing season is very short. Yet there is a wide variety of plant life, with different species in bloom throughout the summer. Bunchberry, the Canadian dogwood, covers great stretches, while the pipsissewa, trillium, and pyrola are found in all the dense woods. There are a host of other flowers, including no less than 36 kinds of orchids flourishing in their natural surroundings. There are also a few unusual members of the floral population, such as the devil's club. Well known in the Pacific Northwest, it also grows on Isle Royale, hundreds of miles away from its native range. But probably no other plants are more generally enjoyed by park visitors than the thriving blueberries, raspberries, strawberries, thimbleberries, or pin cherries, and their fruit.

Since there are 15 miles of fairly deep water separating the main island from the nearest point on the mainland, the wildlife on the island has had to pass this barrier. At first thought it would seem to be a severe hindrance. Yet in the very cold winter of 1912 there was an ice bridge to Canada, and moose migrated to Isle Royale in considerable numbers. They seem to have taken the place of the caribou that inhabited the island until about 30 years ago. Whether the beavers, coyotes, minks, weasles, muskrats, red squirrels, and snowshoe rabbits found here came over a frozen lake surface at some time in the past is not clear. However, the more than 200 species of birds that fly about the island fail to find the lake waters an obstruction.

How do human visitors get to the park? Only by boat. The headquarters are on Mott Island, on the outer chain along 13-mile-long Rock Harbor at the northeast end of the island. There is a boat to and from Copper Harbor, 56 miles, and Houghton, 73 miles away on U.S. 41 in the western peninsula of Michigan. Rock Harbor Lodge lies across Rock Harbor, and about 4 miles up the opposite shore from the headquarters.

There is another lodge at Windigo at the head of Washington Harbor at the opposite end of the main island. There is also boat service at this point to and from Grand Portage, 25 miles away, and located about 4 miles off U.S. 61 at the extreme northeastern tip of Minnesota. Cars must be left at these mainland points, for there are no roads and no vehicles of any sort in the park.

Visitors go to Isle Royale principally to hike, boat, fish, and camp. There are 80 miles of foot trails which reach to the larger lakes, the mine ruins, landmarks, fire towers, and camp sites. Some stretches are primitive, but all paths are well marked. Longest of them is the Greenstone Ridge Trail stretching 30-odd miles from the tip of Scoville Point down the backbone of the island to Windigo at the far end. A week or ten days can readily be given to this trip, for there is excellent fishing in lakes along the trail, and there are side paths to the Lake Superior shore and to abandoned mines. There are three campgrounds beside this main trail, at Lakes Chickenbone, Hatchet, and Desor.

Yet these, and additional campgrounds at nine other

points reached by both trail and boat, are, like the trails, also somewhat primitive. Campers had thus better be experienced and self-reliant. Camp equipment should be reliable and sufficient, for this is wilderness indeed. There should also be ample warm clothing and bedding, for nights can be cool and even crisp. The park season is principally from late June through Labor Day.

BIG BEND

SEVERAL hundred miles back from its mouth in the Gulf of Mexico, the Rio Grande River makes a long, right-angled bend. It thus manages to take a huge bite, amounting to several thousand square miles, from territory that would otherwise be Mexican, and add it to that of the United States. And much of this vast area is more typical of the land south of the border than it is of the better-known parts of our own land.

Near the angular point of this big bend the area is one of sharp contrasts. There are harsh, rocky highlands, mixed with colorful, arid plains, and Nature has thrust up bold mountains and then cut deep valleys through them. It is a grim land, yet the Indians at one time inhabited it, and left the remains of sandals, baskets, and other possessions in caves in which they had lived, and arrow points and grinding stones beside their former camp sites.

189

The Spanish conquerors gave this region quite a little attention 4 centuries ago, and the patient padres maintained missions there for the Apache Indians who then lived in this Big Bend country. It came into the possession of Texas in 1836, and became a part of the United States when Texas was annexed in 1845. By then this section had become isolated and forsaken. The Rangers had a severe brush with Indian bands there along the river in 1863, and its mountainsides and deep canyons later became a refuge for cattle rustlers. It fell to the lot of another Ranger, E. E. Townsend, to trail such outlaws across its sun-blistered plains and waterless uplands. But the forbidding land made a deep impression on this stalwart Texan. He felt that so majestic and unusual a spread of country deserved to be kept in its untamed, natural state. After some years of effort, his fellow Texans caught his enthusiasm. The state set apart $1,500,000, and the title to land held by several hundred owners was assembled and donated to the federal government. Congress had sanctioned preservation of this region in 1935, and in 1944 Big Bend National Park was established.

The 692,304 acres within its boundaries stretch for 107 miles along the winding Rio Grande, which has

Western Ways Photo

Above: The water in the foreground is the Rio Grande River, an indication of the size of Santa Elena Canyon, which it has cut over the ages in Big Bend National Park. *Below left:* In Isle Royale National Park you travel either by boat or on foot or horseback. *Below right:* A view on tranquil Isle Royale out over Duncan Bay toward Lake Superior beyond.

Photos by W. Ray Scott–National Park Concessions, Inc.

Florida State News Bureau

Above: The infinite sweep of saw-grass meadows dotted with palm trees gives Everglades National Park a primitive beauty. Much of its area is water or swampy jungle. *Right:* Our newest park, in the Virgin Islands, is a tropical paradise, with much of its beauty along the ocean front, where the glistening beaches prove highly inviting.

Photo by Fritz Henle

cut three spectacular canyons, all within the preserve. Of these, the first as one descends the river is the Santa Elena at the western tip of the property, where the stream has swung past the great Mesa de Anguila. Its nearly vertical cliffs rise some 1500 feet above the present channel. Furthest east is Boquillas Canyon, where the river has knifed its way through the Sierra del Carmen range. These two wonder spots may be reached by improved roads. The third, Mariscal Canyon, is at the very peak of the mighty bend, and can be visited only on foot or horseback.

Almost in the center of the roughly triangular park are the Chisos Mountains. Certain of the peaks rise to elevations close to 8000 feet, while the broader valleys are carpeted with trees. There are actually four general types of plant communities. One is the typical desert "scrub," found usually in the lowlands, with a partial cover of creosotebush, yucca, cactus, and other similar growth. On the lower mountain slopes are stands of the small, bushy, nut-bearing piñon pine and the juniper. Higher up on the shoulders of the Chisos and other ranges are sparse but vigorous growths of ponderosa pine, Douglas fir, Arizona cypress, and the quaking aspen. About springs and water holes, and along the Rio Grande's banks, there are many moisture-demanding plants. Among them is the Palmer cottonwood, and a very large reed not unlike bamboo.

Of the manifold animal life that embraces at least 60 mammals, the most plentiful of the larger creatures are the mule and the white-tailed, or "flagtail," deer. Best chances of seeing them are during their grazing periods in early morning and evening hours. There are some antelope, and very often one or several of these fleet-footed beasts will try to match their speed with that of an automobile. Occasionally the cry of a mountain lion will ring out during the night, but both the lion and the Mexican black bear that also inhabit the Chisos uplands are seldom encountered. Another very unusual animal living in these same hills is the Texas peccary—the javelina, or "wild hog." These blackish gray swine, about three feet long and 18 inches to the shoulders, have a pair of tusks, and can be dangerous if cornered. There are, of course, the toads, lizards, and other types of desert reptiles, and also a very large variety of the more common birds. This is hardly a barren or an empty land.

Yet to many the rocks are of even greater interest than the animals, or the more than 1100 kinds of vegetation within park bounds. The area has had a very violent past, in part volcanic, and many rock strata are highly folded, tilted, shattered, and eroded. Some layers now stand on end, others are lopsided, and a few have been rolled upside down or thrust to points far from where they normally should be. It is thus an amateur geologist's—a "rock hound's"—paradise. There are more than a thousand square miles to explore, and the possible finds run all the way from tiny bits of agate to sections of petrified tree trunk as much as 10 feet in diameter. Some of these once-great logs, their woody fibers now replaced by beautifully grained stone, may originally have been more than 100 feet long. They are usually broken up into many sections, and the exposed faces of these segments often have the veining and warm colors of the most beautiful onyx.

The rocks which form the park's mountains were first laid down beneath some ancient sea. They are consequently filled with the remains of former marine life, such as sea shells and the hardened traces of plants and animals. Some rather amazing finds of this sort have been made, among them enormous oyster and clam shells. One of the latter was no less than 4 feet long. However, the rocks are interesting, too, merely to look at. With a great expenditure of effort, Nature has cut deep canyons, and formed towering cliffs, columns, spires, and buttresses, with highly colored walls, and affording magnificent views.

The park lies south of U.S. 90, and is some 290 miles from El Paso, and about 600 from Brownsville, as well as from Dallas or Fort Worth. There are two entrances, both from the north. One is at Persimmon Gap, 39 miles south of Marathon, via State Route 227. It is an added 29 miles in to the headquarters, and 10 miles more to the recreational center in the Chisos Mountains Basin. The other is 81 miles below Alpine, on State Route 118. From there it is 23 miles to headquarters, and 27 to the Basin area. Both routes are by paved and improved roads.

There are cabin accommodations at the center in the mountains, and also a store, restaurant, service station, and saddle horse corral. Additional but somewhat limited accommodations can be found at the Hot Springs near Boquillas Canyon in the extreme southeast corner of the park. However, Big Bend is primarily for those who like to rough it. Camping is encouraged, and there are three campgrounds available.

The park is open the year round, and is sunny and dry from fall through the spring. The rains come during the summer and bring both growth and blossoms to their finest, but they are over by mid-September.

The temperature runs from 60° to 85° in the warmer months, and from 40° to 60° in midwinter.

Like Glacier National Park in Montana, Big Bend lies on an international boundary. Boquillas Village in Mexico is almost directly across the Rio Grande from the lookout atop the walls of the famous canyon similarly named. It is still hoped that someday our neighbor nation to the south will set aside territory below the river so there may be a second International Peace Park.

EVERGLADES

THERE is an immense area, which takes in most of the southern tip of Florida south of Lake Okeechobee, that was known to the Indians as "Pahayokee," or grassy waters. Our name for these endless marshlands is the Everglades. They are unique, for there is nothing like them at any other point within the United States or its possessions. While they appear to be a limitless and largely worthless wilderness, it seemed prudent for many reasons that a portion of this vast region be preserved. An investigation was begun in 1929, and a park authorized in 1934. It finally came into being in 1947, when Florida deeded a very large tract to the federal government, and made funds available for acquiring other neighboring territory. There are now 1,258,361 acres within park limits, making this next to the newest park our third largest, exceeded only by Yellowstone and Mount McKinley.

Shaped like a broken arrowhead, the preserve takes in the tip of the Florida peninsula and bordering waters. Its northern boundaries follow along, and at two points reach to, U.S. 41, the famous Tamiami Trail. About 25 miles west of Miami the line drops south and goes west of the city of Homestead to the entrance in the Royal Palm Area. Turning east again, the park domain extends to U.S. 1, and follows that highway over the spit of land to the Florida Keys. It then takes in the waters and countless islets in Florida Bay, passes around Cape Sable, and runs northwest through the Gulf of Mexico. It thus gives protection to the shore waters along the mangrove jungles almost as far as the resort town of Everglades. Certain salt-water regions are included for the better protection of important bird rookeries, where rare waterfowl nest.

Land access to the park is from Florida City on U.S. 1, over State Route 27. There is an improved road for motor vehicles running some 33 miles through the sanctuary to Flamingo on Cape Sable at the southwest corner bordering on Florida Bay. A tour by means of this safe, dry thoroughfare will give a good impression of the wonders in all parts of the park.

About 2 miles inside the entrance is the Anhinga Trail, an elevated walk from which wildlife can be viewed at close range but with perfect safety. Within this park there are panthers, deer, bears, big snakes, and alligators. Close by it is the Gumbo Limbo Trail. A naturalist conducts parties over this fairly limited course, after having let them first have a look at the fine exhibits in the Royal Palm Ranger Station. Just to the west of this latter there is a picnic ground. Five miles beyond, at Cypress Head, is another raised walk leading into a typical cypress and hammock "island." At End o'Glades, at the edge of the mangrove forests, there is an observation tower for a lookout over the two quite different types of countryside.

Twenty-five miles along this roadway, at West Lake Pond, there is a cruise-boat landing, and an excellent opportunity to view both the junglelike mangrove thickets and the teeming waterfowl. It is only 4 miles more to Coot Bay, a recreation center, where there are refreshments, boats, bait, and access to good fishing. Flamingo, at the end of the road, also has charter boats, fishing skiffs, and bait. There is an old commercial fish company hut on exhibit here, a picnic area, and camping is permitted. Occasionally, when the unsurfaced dirt road beyond is safe, it is possible to drive several additional miles out onto Cape Sable.

There are two quite distinct seasons in the park.

They are generally spoken of as "summer" and "winter," although the first extends from May 1 to the end of November, and the other from the beginning of December through April. More people visit the park during this colder period, since that is the principal tourist season. The weather then is pleasant, reasonably cool, and rain is scarce, with sometimes a month between showers. The trees and shrubs stay green, although the sedge and other grasses turn brown. The bird life is very active, with many visitors from the north and many of the local varieties gathered about the sloughs, lakes, and water areas.

There are several large, showy birds in this region, and certain of them nest in their breeding places at this time of year. Most are wading birds, such as the egrets, the herons, ibis, and roseate spoonbills. There are also other kinds of waterfowl, such as the gulls or the brown pelicans, that are commonly seen and heard. Fishing is fairly good during this cooler weather, but the water can be decidedly rough at times.

Summer in southern Florida is the rainy season. This is due to heavy showers rather than because of all-day storms. Sometimes there is lightning, but not always, yet the rain can fall in torrents in either event. As this warmer part of the year moves ahead, the thermometer mounts, and so does the sticky humidity. The continuing wet weather tends to raise the water level, until four fifths of the almost 2000 square miles of park surface is submerged. The insects become numerous and annoying. There is also a storm period during August and September, when those attempting extended trips within the reservation are asked to take radios so they may receive hurricane warnings. Unfortunately, this is the better fishing season, and park waters are usually calmer at this time of year. The vegetation is lush and the Everglades grasses very green, for this is their growing season. Yet the wildlife is widely distributed and but little seen again until late fall.

Because of these generally unfavorable conditions, the number of visitors falls off rapidly as the temperature begins its climb. Consequently the park staff is cut to a skeleton crew, and the services offered within its bounds have to be reduced. Every effort is made, however, to give the visitors the best of attention throughout the year, for the park is always open.

Those who enjoy boating have two opportunities for guided trips through the park's mystic maze of waterways. One is offered by Audubon Wildlife Tours, and starts from National Audubon Society's headquarters in Miami. There are both one- and two-day trips, which cross the peninsula to Duck Rock in the Ten Thousand Islands section along the Gulf coast. A second day is spent in Corkscrew Swamp in the same vicinity. Everglades Transway Service operates its boats from bases within the park, and their much shorter excursions last only 1½ to 2 hours.

VIRGIN ISLANDS

About 1400 miles south and a little east of New York there is an island archipelago which Columbus discovered and named. He called this group the Virgin Islands in honor of St. Ursula and her 11,000 virgin companions in martyrdom. Of its 50 or more islands and islets, part came into the possession of Great Britain, while the remainder were taken over by the Danes in 1687. For nearly 2½ centuries they were known as the Danish West Indies, and in 1917 were purchased by the United States.

Of the American Virgins, the three largest are known as St. Croix, St. Thomas—on which is the islands' capital city, Charlotte Amalie—and St. John. These last two are separated only by 2-mile-wide Pillsbury Sound, while St. Croix lies about 40 miles south of the others. St. John, smallest of them, with an area of just over 19 square miles, has the least population.

First permanent settlement on it was made in 1717, when twenty planters and five soldiers landed there. They fortified a cone-shaped hill which thrusts out into roomy Coral Bay, on the east end of the island, and soon drove the few British away. Fortberg Hill, which they had chosen for their stronghold, was high enough so they might see all who tried to approach their new home from any side. This no doubt helped them to keep possession, and in just a few years all available land had been taken over for sugar plantations. There were periods of prosperity, and then of trouble, chiefly with the slaves that manned the large estates. Finally, about the middle of the 1800s, slavery was abolished in the Danish West Indies. The cost of producing sugar then increased to a point where the plantations were closed, the planters left the island, and its fields returned to "bush," as the native tropical vegetation is locally known.

While the larger islands of St. Croix and St. Thomas have changed markedly, especially since they were joined to the United States, St. John has pretty much returned to its original, unspoiled beauty. Although visitors to it have been fairly few over the years, those who have come to know its great charm have felt that it should be preserved. One of our established parks had a distinct tropical setting. But it lay far to the west, on two of the Hawaiian Islands. Its volcanic wonders are indeed outstanding, yet so far away that but few make the effort to visit it. There were other tropical gems that were closer to the bulk of our population. And they lay in a region becoming ever more popular as a vacation land.

Consequently, almost 20 years ago, some consideration was given to the possibility of establishing a national sanctuary at some point in the Virgin group. Even then the choice favored St. John, because it was closer to the tropical paradise it had once been. But with the coming of World War II the scheme was set aside, yet not by any means forgotten. Interest finally began to grow again, and was much increased in 1954 through the support of Laurance S. Rockefeller. His father, John D. Rockefeller, Jr., had been very staunch in his aid of the national park program, and had made large donations to help establish Grand Teton and Great Smoky Mountains parks. His son, who is carrying on his father's interest in park matters, purchased some 5000 acres of land on St. John. This he very generously turned over to the federal government. It then took two years to make plans and to obtain passage of needed legislation by Congress. But the bill, signed by President Eisenhower in August 1956, made Virgin Islands National Park the twenty-ninth area to be raised to membership in a very select group.

However, this newest park, like all the others, has its own unusual and unique qualities. It provides tropical loveliness of a sort unmatched anywhere else in the public domain. In area, this may ever be one of our smallest parks. Yet, as it becomes better known, it need never lack visitors.

St. John Island, while rather irregular in shape, is about 9 miles long and nearly 5 miles wide. It rises abruptly from the sea in a series of steep, sharp mountains and deep, narrow valleys. Of its 12,000 acres, only about four fifths have so far been taken into the park. Some 750 people still make their homes on the island. So a strip along Coral Bay and another block in the southwest corner where there are also settlements and cleared fields have not been included. Within park bounds is Bordeaux Mountain, whose 1277-foot summit is the highest point. The preserve stretches along the entire rugged north shore, takes in the center of the island, and spread out again to include much of the southern coast.

Most of this area is covered by a second-growth, tropical forest. A portion of this forest was first cut to make clearings in which to plant sugar cane. Then the trees and brush were pretty much stripped from the remainder to produce charcoal with which to boil cane juice into molasses and sugar. But during the past 100 years the forest growth has been well restored. Little St. John has a very great variety of woody plants. There are no less than 154 types of trees, a very great assortment, together with some 72 kinds of shrubs and many sorts of vines. This small bit of land surrounded by whole oceans of water even has 8 sorts of cactus. And they are not all small-sized plants by any means, for one variety grows 20 feet tall and looks very much like the organpipe cactus in the deserts of our Southwest. Most common among the trees are the cinnamon-bay, breadfruit, fig, guava, mahogany, mango, mangrove, palm, sea grape, and soursop. The flamboyant, hibiscus, and bougainvillea, together with other flowering shrubs, are very common and make the mountainsides bright with color.

Wildlife, as is true on other West Indies islands, is very limited. The mongoose, one of the few wild creatures, was brought from Asia to kill rats but is now a nuisance, for it also kills chickens, birds, and the smaller animals. There are a few lizards of limited size, but no snakes. Flies and mosquitoes are also rather scarce. But bird life is abundant, with many visitors from the North American mainland and numerous native species. There are few parakeets and great numbers of interesting waterfowl. Deep-sea fish that may be caught just offshore include barracuda, bonita, dolphin, kingfish, sailfish, tarpon, and tuna. There are highly interesting and very colorful small tropical fish along the beaches and shoal waters. And the glistening white beach sands are strewn with countless shells, even the large, spiral king and queen conch shells.

The various parts of the park may be reached by car or on foot, on horseback, or by boat. There are ruins of manor houses, sugar mills, forts, and batteries to be visited, and even rocks covered with the strange picture writing of the Carib Indians. Park roads are still somewhat primitive, and trails and bridle paths will be improved and extended as time goes on. There is ample shade to temper the sun's heat, and the ever-blowing trade winds help to keep the temperature very even. The average throughout the year is 78°, with a difference of only about 6° between summer and winter. The lowest thermometer reading ever recorded is 69°, and the highest 91°. It is particularly lovely along the many beaches, where the swimming is excellent, and there is a whole world of underwater wonders for skin-divers and aqua-lung enthusiasts to explore.

Charlotte Amalie on neighboring St. Thomas has regular ship and plane connection with the United States mainland. There is frequent mail and passenger service to St. John by means of government-owned and-operated launches. Tourist accommodations can be found on the larger island, but they are also available on St. John at Caneel, Trunk, Cruz, and Coral bays.

First visitors were welcomed to this newest of our national parks in December 1956.

THESE OTHER NATIONAL AREAS
DESERVE YOUR ATTENTION

WHILE this Real Book deals solely with the national parks, we must not forget the 150 or more other areas administered by the National Park Service. They, too, form a distinct part of our fine heritage, and many of them lie in the same vicinity as the parks and can be visited along with them.

While there seem to be 12 different types of these areas, some of them have close similarity. One thing they do have in common is the qualities of national significance. Thus they have more than state or local interest, and are worthy of our attention and of a visit. But since their number is so great, it is impossible to describe or even list all of them in this volume.

The most numerous class is the national monuments. They are of wide variety, and range from such natural objects as a section of the Badlands in South

Dakota, or a portion of the redwood forests, the Muir Woods in California, to such man-made structures as famous Fort Laramie in Wyoming.

There are military parks at Gettysburg, Vicksburg, Shiloh, and elsewhere; while the areas about Richmond which figured in that city's siege are spoken of as a battlefield park. The site of the famous encounter between the 7th Cavalry and Sitting Bull and his band is called Custer Battlefield National Monument.

The national memorials are also of several types. Probably the three most famous are the Washington Monument and the shrines to Jefferson and Lincoln in our national capital. Across the Potomac from the city, near the grave of the Unknown Soldier in the National Cemetery, is the lovely Lee Mansion, while a quite different sort of memorial is that made up of the magnificent carved heads of four of the presidents high on the side of Mount Rushmore in South Dakota.

The historical parks are typified by the one near Saratoga Springs, New York, where the defeat of the British under Burgoyne marked a definite turning point in the Revolution. Probably the best known and most frequently visited is Independence Hall in Philadelphia which, with its surroundings, is designated a Historical Park Project. Of a somewhat different kind is the Hopewell Village National Historic Site, a little blast-furnace town of an earlier time, which lies about 40 miles northwest of the Cradle of Our Liberties.

Presumably the most visited of all of the many spots under federal control is the huge national recreational area at Lake Mead, stretching along the Colorado River for many miles in the states of Nevada and Arizona. Many, many thousands, too, travel over the two great national parkways. The Blue Ridge joins the Shenandoah and the Great Smoky parks, while Natchez Trace helps to perpetuate the famous trail that connected Tennessee and Mississippi, and played so great a role in the winning of that frontier.

Thus we have in addition to the 29 parks more than 150 other localities of wide variety and interest deserving of a visit. For your use, the National Park Service has prepared informational leaflets, folders, and booklets upon each of the areas under its direction. There are also maps and other general data in printed form available at cost, which is described in a check list of *National Park Service Publication*, a copy of which may be had free from the Superintendent of Documents, Government Printing Office, Washington 25, D. C. From it you may select information to aid in planning countless interesting trips.

OTHER BOOKS ABOUT THE
NATIONAL PARKS

EXPLORING OUR NATIONAL PARKS—by Devereux
Butcher (Houghton Mifflin Co.)

STEVE MATHER OF THE NATIONAL PARKS—by
Robert Shankland (Alfred A. Knopf, Inc.)

THE NATIONAL PARKS; WHAT THEY MEAN TO YOU
AND ME—by Freeman Tilden (Alfred A. Knopf, Inc.)

PARK RANGER—by C. B. Colby (Coward-McCann, Inc.)

AMERICA'S NATIONAL PARKS—by Nelson Beecher Keyes
(Doubleday & Co., Inc.)

212

INDEX

Acadia, 111–16

Antelope, 64, 192; pronghorn, 34

Antelope Spring, 73

Appalachian Trail, 150–51, 164

Argall, Captain Samuel, 111

Badger Pass Ski Center, 39

Bats, at Carlsbad Caverns, 156, 162

Bears, black, 33, 81, 89, 101, 154, 167, 169, 178, 192; brown, 33, 46, 144; cinnamon, 33; grizzlies, 33, 81, 107

Beaver, 81, 89, 186

Big Bend, 189–95

Blue Ridge Parkway, 155

Bridalveil Falls, 37

Bridger, James (Jim), 30

Bromide Hill, legend of, 74

Bryce Canyon, 123, 128, 136–41

Buffalo, 34, 64

Buffalo Spring, 73

Cadillac, Sieur de la Mothe, 112

Caribou, 106

Carlsbad Caverns, 156–62, 169

Carson, Christopher (Kit), 85

Cascade Range, 48, 54, 97, 178

Cedar Breaks National Monument, 128, 140–41

Champlain, Samuel de, 111

Cinder Cone, 99, 100

Cliff Palace, 67, 68, 70

Colorado River, 15

Colter, John, 30, 142

Colter's Hell, 30

Continental Divide, 77, 79, 84

Crater Lake, 16, 48, 54–59, 97

Deer, 64, 89; black-tailed, 101; mule, 34, 46, 81, 101, 127, 144; whitetail, 81, 154, 167, 192

Denali, "home of the sun," 104

Disney, Walt, 177

Eagle, 34; bald, 101, 145; golden, 46

213

Elk, or wapiti, 34, 64, 81, 89, 144; Roosevelt, or Olympic, 177
Emmons Glacier, 49
Estes, Joel, 85
Everglades, 196–201

Fall River Road, 87
Fees, why charged, 26
Fishing, why permitted, 28
Flowstone, 63, 170
Fort Smith, Arkansas, 13, 14
Frostwork deposits, 63

General Grant National Park, 43
General Sherman Tree, 44
Geysers, in Yellowstone, 31, 32
Glacier National Park, 77–83, 195
Glaciers, on Mount Rainier, 49–51; in Glacier Park, 77; on Mount McKinley, 105, 106; on Mount Olympus, 179
Goats, mountain, 81
Going-to-the-Sun Highway, 79, 82
Grand Canyon, 117–23, 128, 136
Grand Teton, 142–48
Great Smoky Mountains, 149–55

Haleakala, 93, 94
Halemaumau, 92
Half Dome, 37
Havasupai Indians, 118
Hawaii National Park, 16, 90–96, 97
Hot Springs National Park, 130–35
Hot Springs Reservation, 14, 131
Hunting, why restricted, 28

Isle Royale, 182–88

Jackson Hole, 143

Kaibab Suspension Bridge, 121
Kilauea, 92
Kings Canyon, 42–47

Lake Mead, 118
Lassen Peak, 48
Lassen, Peter, 98
Lassen Volcanic National Park, 97–103
Lava flows, 91–93, 98
Lion, mountain, 81–89, 127, 192
Longs Peak, 85

Mammoth Cave, 169–74
Mancos River, 66, 69
Mariposa Grove, big trees, 36, 38
Mauna Loa, 90, 92, 98

214

Mesa Verde, 66–71
Moose, 34, 81, 107, 144, 186
Mount Desert Island, 111, 112, 113, 115
Mount McKinley, 16, 104–10
Mount Rainier, 16, 48–53, 97
Mount Rushmore, 65
Mount Whitney, 43, 45

National Park Service, organized, 16; purposes, 16; men and women of, 18–21; things to know about, 23; and park facilities, 26
National Parks, in other lands, 23; how regulated, 23; differences in, 24; how established, 24; differences from other national areas, 25
Naturalists, 20
Never Summer Mountains, 86
Nisqually Glacier, 50

Old Faithful, famous geyser, 32
Olympic, 175–81
Ouachita Mountains, 14, 130

Platt National Park, 72–76
Platt, Orville Hitchcock, 73
Powell, John Wesley, 119, 124

Rangers, duties of, 20
Reindeer, 107

Rockefeller, John D., Jr., 147, 150, 204
Rockefeller, Laurance S., 204
Rocky Mountain National Park, 84–89

St. John Island, 202, 203, 205
Sequoia, 16, 42–47
Sheep, bighorn mountain, 34, 81, 89, 145; Dall, 107
Shenandoah, 155, 163–68
Sierra Nevada Mountains, 37, 42, 45
Skiing, 40, 46, 52, 58, 102, 148, 168
Skyline Drive, 164, 165
Spotswood, Alexander, 163
Spruce Tree House, 67
Stalactites, 63, 159, 170
Stalagmites, 63, 159, 170
Steel, William Gladstone, 55
Sulphur Springs Reservation, 73
Sulphur Works, 100, 102
Surfbird, elusive, 108

Townsend, Ranger, E. E., 190
Trail Ridge Road, 86
Travertine Creek, 73, 74
Tuolumne Meadows, 39
Turkey, wild, 154, 167

Virgin Islands, 16, 202–8

215

Wapiti, or elk, 34, 81, 144
Washburn, Mr. and Mrs. Bradford, 106
Waterton-Glacier International Peace Park, 77, 82, 83
Waterton Lakes National Park, 77, 82, 83
White, James (Jim), 157
Wildlife, abundance or scarcity of, 27; Yellowstone sanctuary for, 33; extensive in Glacier, 81; in Rocky Mountain Park, 88; dearth of in Hawaii, 95, and in Virgin Islands, 206; in Mount McKinley Park, 106; in Grand Teton, 144; Olympic outstanding refuge for, 177–78
Wind Cave, 60–65
Wootton, Richens Lacy (Uncle Dick), 85

Yellowstone, 15, 30–35, 48, 97, 147
Yellowstone River, 33
Yosemite, 15, 36–41; Falls, 38

Zion, 123, 124–29, 136